Epitaph to 'Nickle Eck'

Childhood Mischief in Wartime Birmingham

by

Eric Yates

Illustrated by John Ashton
www.artashton.co.uk

Cover photograph 'Evacuation from Snow Hill Station' courtesy of
Birmingham Archives & Heritage. Donor Ref BAH:
Misc.Photos/Home Front/ Box 2/15 (110/2223)'
ISBN-13: 978-1505435429
ISBN-10: 1505435420

DEDICATION

This book is dedicated to Eric's grandsons
Jacob and Aram McCormack.
It is also dedicated, with love, to Eric.

ACKNOWLEDGMENTS

We extend a huge debt of gratitude to Eric's widow, Lutena, for the patience and dedication she has shown to bring this unusual book to fruition.

Eric wrote these wonderful stories in 2004 but not until last year, at Lutena's request, did John provide detailed information for the Foreword and his personal and painful memories for 'Family Life with Dad'. Sadly neither of these highly individual men are still with us.

For ten years Eric's stories were put aside but, following his death in 2012, Lutena determinedly took on the task of editing and creating a complete book – not only bringing the stories into proper order but, referring to us, tirelessly checking and re-checking the facts, dates, names, and places as far as possible. She remained enthusiastic throughout, despite the highs and lows that always occur with a project such as this.

This book was a labour of love for Lutena and she has done it brilliantly. Because of her, the book will be a permanent homage to her beloved husband Eric and his brother John – who we suspect continue happily causing havoc together for eternity. Both of us thank you from the bottom of our hearts for ensuring our loved ones live on.

Pat Yates & Sue Ridley

(John's widow and the boys' younger sister)

i

*

I would like to add my personal thanks to Pat and Sue, who have been endlessly encouraging and supportive throughout the past year, and also to my many friends who have shown such interest, in particular Ann Bentley and Liz Powell who gave invaluable predictions and advice when I needed it, and to Yvonne Knapman and Erica Anderson for patiently solving my numerous technical problems.

I also owe special thanks to my friend, professional artist John Ashton, not only for giving up his valuable time providing additional drawings at short notice, but for caricaturing Eric and John so perfectly. Eric would have wholeheartedly approved as he and John were drinking partners and great mates!

Lutena Yates

November 2014

PART ONE

Epitaph to 'Nickle Eck'

FOREWORD

Our paternal grandmother, Laura Annie Pratt, believed to be of Russian extraction, was born in Staffordshire in 1857 and was of 'the old school' attending an Academy for Ladies, being taught French and music amongst other genteel subjects. She was very musical, using her talent to earn money by accompanying the early silent films.

Laura married an educated man, George Mallen Yates, who became the Assistant Overseer/Rate Collector of Brierley Hill in the Black Country, and they produced three sons, Leon George, Cyril Ronald, and Herbert Basil Hugo, our father. In the 1890s there was a huge scandal in the family when our grandfather absconded from his post of Town Clerk with five thousand pounds, which was a great deal of money in those days. The whole family made a dash to book for Canada on an ocean liner but, unfortunately for them, long-distance radio was introduced at that time and the Police sent a signal to Canada where Grandad was duly arrested on arrival, so the depleted family had to return to the UK. No more is known about George Mallon Yates - except that in 1916 Dad's first marriage certificate describes him as 'Deceased'.

It was the early 1900s and life was very hard for Grandma, who had to feed, clothe and educate her sons. So, being an enterprising woman she rented a small hotel from where she ran a discreet but very popular brothel. The customers were usually regular callers and, because there were many ladies desperate to earn an income, the local officials turned a blind eye as employment was very difficult to come by. It was noted that the local police officers were keen customers, on the principle that 'one good turn deserves another'.

Dad was born in 1897, and eight years later he had to earn money carrying suitcases on Snow Hill Station in Birmingham for one penny a time, giving his meagre earnings to his mother for food. In fact, Dad had to support his mother, Laura Annie, as his elder brother was killed near Lille in 1915 and the middle brother, Cyril (who became a piano tuner), was blind. Grandma continued to live with our family until she died in 1943.

Dad was a clever man and a well-respected toolmaker. When sober he was a private, mild-mannered person of solitary habits but the effect of draught beer triggered his overwhelming bitterness. He was only sixteen when he started up his own engineering business in Smethwick, which was successful until World War I broke out in 1914 when he was unable to obtain the necessary metal to continue but, as he was a highly skilled toolmaker, he managed to get work in a factory. He used to walk miles to work, with cardboard in his worn-out shoes, having no spare money for either food or bus fare.

In early 1915 Dad met Beatrice Rose Ingram, a young woman who worked in the same factory, and they married in September 1916. They had a son, Herbert Ronald Hugo – forever afterwards known as Ronnie. Tragically, when Ronnie was very young, his mother died in extreme agony from an inoperable brain tumour. Outside her hospital ward Dad heard her screams, gradually subsiding as the morphine took over. Thereafter, Grandma took over the care of Ronnie.

It was later when, working for BSA (the Birmingham Small Arms factory) in Armoury Road, Small Heath, Dad met our mother, Marjorie Poole, in Smethwick where she was working for her father, a master butcher and a giant of a man, in his shop 'Poole's Pedigree Pigs'. Mom was a very bright and attractive young woman with pretty, light auburn hair and a pale skin; she was of medium height and, in her younger days, really slim with very good legs. Dad was about 5'9", dark haired and clean-shaven. He was a smoker, always tidily dressed and never seen without a collar and tie. Following their marriage in 1930, Dad formed an engineering company which went bankrupt as the timing coincided with the ferocities of the financial meltdown in the 1930s. The regular arrival of children during his subsequent marriage to Mom did little to improve his disposition. Dad frequently remarked that 'clever women don't have babies' – which puzzled me for several years as I observed that not to be the case.

Our parents took up a tenancy of a semi-detached council house – 85 Broomhall Crescent, Hall Green, Birmingham. John was born there in 1931 and I was born in 1933.

As the Great Depression of the 1930s developed, our parents had to give up the tenancy in Hall Green to relocate to Mom's parents, who had a huge three-storey house in Small Heath, which was in sight of Birmingham City Football Club. It was a very run down area and the house had a large gravel frontage, adjacent to the main road leading to Birmingham City centre, with buses, tramcars, and other vehicles passing all day long. The house required loads of coal for the open fires, boiler, bedrooms and open cooker. This was obtained from a coal yard half a mile away, so John had to help load up an old pram and struggle to push it back home up a long hill. On Saturdays, during football matches, the frontage of the house was packed with cars and motor bikes, so we boys would ask the drivers for a penny to look after their vehicles which gave us pocket money for the following fortnight.

As the Depression eased, Dad had a steady job and we moved to 20 Dalston Road, Acocks Green, Birmingham, from where John and I eventually went to school, firstly attending the local primary school at Acocks Green. When he was eleven, John was sent to Bordesley Green Technical College which suited his talents, but I won a scholarship to Yardley Grammar School as I was the academic son, my siblings being very skilled on the technical and practical side. Instead of showing fatherly pride in my achievement, Dad used to enjoy mocking me as I set off for school weighed down with my satchel full of books, and I was mortified to be mercilessly teased by pupils for being 'the odd one out'. Dad never gave either of us any praise or encouragement; when only twelve John was skilled at making radios, but Dad showed total disinterest. In retrospect I think he always felt he too could have been a great achiever, given the opportunity, and was embittered by his early life and subsequent lack of formal education. He obviously had a very good brain, which we all inherited, but could never achieve his potential. He once told John he gave us common names as he knew we would only end up working in factories. Little did he know!

When World War II broke out BSA appointed Dad Chief Quality Control Inspector, which was a very important role as accuracy was crucial for the making of machine tools for weapons. Because this function was so important Dad was in protected employment, mainly supervising a workforce of women at the time, so not called up for the services. It is said that Dad was very highly thought of, his word being law regarding whether an item should be passed or scrapped. He was also able to patent engineering machinery.

On 19th November 1940 there was a bombing raid, the most severe attack on Birmingham during the course of the war. It was centred on industrial sites, and the BSA factory had a direct hit causing loss of rifle production for three months. The upper floor fell on to the women working below, killing them all. This was hushed up at the time because of morale; it distressed Dad terribly. Subsequently, BSA moved out to the then leafy-suburbs of Bordesley Green, where Dad continued to work until he retired.

*

Our step-brother Ronnie lived with us for a time at Dalston

Road but, being fourteen years our senior, he was a bad influence on us boys. Ronnie was a very jovial but disreputable character, spending his life thieving, falsifying documents, and swindling book makers; he spent a few years in prison for theft, which added to Dad's woes.

Ronnie regularly went dog racing and often took John with him; very often he lost all his money to the bookmakers. Once, as he had no money to pay for a bus ride, he nonchalantly stole a motor bike from the parking area and rode himself and John home, abandoning the motor bike nearby. The local police identified the bike by the registration number and returned it to its owner.

In 1939 Ronnie married Sarah Ellen Lawton, known as 'Nellie', and they had six children. He was called up for WWII and he enrolled in the RAF, but was eventually thrown out as he created chaos with his consistent habit of stealing and selling off wartime equipment. At one time Nellie and the children all stayed with us; Mom welcomed them and did her best, but there was so little room for them they were moved into a hostel before being allocated a council house. Ronnie did settle down for a while to work at a newspaper and was able to produce copper plate writing, creating very good cartoons and posters.

At the end of the war in 1945, there were street parties in all the roads where we lived, and John and I used to collect as much scrap timber as we could find for a celebration fire in our large front garden. Ronnie came round when it was almost dark and added many larger items which he said he had found. The celebration was a huge success and went on well past midnight, with music and dancing around the blazing bonfire. Next morning we awoke to a loud commotion and ran outside to find a crowd of neighbours complaining that all their garden gates had been stolen and used for the fire. The Police were called but were at a loss as to who had stolen the gates, as there were no fingerprints in the ashes. Ronnie kept well out of the way and no-one was ever arrested.

One post-war Christmas the family had little money for much in the way of decorations and trimmings, but Ronnie, John and I went out with our parents on Christmas Eve to buy a few extras for Christmas Day. On the way home, Dad complained that he couldn't see out of the rear view mirror so had to drive using the wing mirrors, which were located well in front of the driver in those days. All was revealed when we arrived home; Ronnie had appropriated a huge Christmas tree and tied it to the rear of the car. Dad was very annoyed, but we had a wonderful time making our own trimmings for the tree.

Ronnie inherited Dad's character and insecurities, becoming morose as he grew older and displayed bouts of weird behaviour, ill-treating Nellie and the family. Fortunately however, most of the siblings were very close and supported each other throughout their lives, sharing their very distressing memories as a form of therapy. Some of them emigrated but kept in touch with their Dad, who died in a London hospital in 1992.

WARTIME RESTRICTIONS

Rationing has often, rather loftily, been written about as a great victory for British organisation and our great sense of 'Fair play'. Where I came from it was a glorious opportunity for barter, black-marketing and profiteering.

Petrol was King, as very little was allocated to the private sector, mainly for doctors and similar professionals. Other recipients were skilled engineers in reserved occupations such as our Dad, a toolmaker, who owned a pre-war Jowett – an unusual possession for a working-class family on a Council Estate. Petrol coupons were almost priceless and a sub-industry of petrol siphoning soon emerged. Unwary small children were taken out at night by their elder brothers, equipped with a can and a length of hosepipe (readily available cut from stirrup pumps which proliferated in wartime). A victim's car would be pre-selected in an unlit street and the hose inserted into the tank, facilitated by the lack of cap-locks or double bends leading to the tank. The youngster would then be given the free end and told to suck hard and push the end into the can when the fluid flowed. This instruction was somewhat superfluous as the watching elders grabbed the hose when the child's eyes opened wide, his face turned a funny colour and he began to choke. A gallon of petrol gained this way was easily sold – sometimes for a whole pound note, a week's beer or a yard of knicker elastic.

The penalty for this type of theft was severe, which is where the use of a disposable urchin came in. If the scavengers were disturbed they fled in different directions leaving the child, coughing and retching, to 'carry the can'. He would be too young to be prosecuted – and probably too ill to testify.

Another source was Industrial petrol, available to essential haulage vehicles and from agricultural equipment. This fuel was dyed a reddish-pink colour and was easily identified if used in private cars, but this did not preclude many embryonic alchemists in Birmingham from adding their favourite ingredient to metamorphose it into liquid gold. Of course there were many accidents, as the highly inflammable mixtures metamorphosed the mixers and their garages into ashes. But, such is progress...

There were many illegalities during the war but we never ran short of rationed items. Our Uncle Alf, Mom's brother, drove a fire engine so petrol coupons for fuel were available to him at all times for such a crucial vehicle and he was never questioned. To conserve fuel all private cars were limited by law to a few coupons each month, but Dad never ran short. Another of Mom's brothers, Uncle Arthur, was a pig farmer living in Coleshill. Meat was restricted to food coupons, as were almost all other food items, but Uncle Arthur would smuggle a piglet into a hidden sty and slaughter it for all the family so there was no shortage of meat - especially at Christmas.

Rationing worked splendidly if the families of a working class council estate understood the basic premise, which was flawed. Bread was not rationed and few families could eat all the bread allowed, but distribution was restricted to only one daily delivery and Mom made sure our family was always at the front of the queue. Therefore, if a family needed extra bread we, the Yates's, honed in on them and began to barter. Mom found that a local family, named Jebb, were supreme champions at eking out the meagre tea ration – which was based on the little-understood fact that very little tea was grown in England, especially in Birmingham.

For my family, Eldorado was gained by the tea ration, which fluctuated sometimes down to two ounces per week. This was a desperate situation as Dad, my elder brother John and I drank only a dark brown brew sweetened with condensed milk (courtesy of the babies) which we regarded as life-enhancing – and chest hair nutrition in later life.

The Jebb family, who lived on tea, had developed a constant brew in a very large teapot throughout the day to sustain family, friends and visitors. Mrs Jebb perfected the art of tea-brewing by the constant addition of hot water to the leaves, which became pallid and wan so one could easily discern the name 'Great Western Railway' on the underside of the cup. Every six hours a single teaspoon of tea would be added to the pot, to maintain its innocence. Any robust visitor, on being presented with a cup of this perpetual liquor, would turn a funny colour – similar to that of the tea. The Yates family, having reluctantly partaken of this brew, struck a bargain with the Jebbs when we discovered they were always short of bread, which we had in abundance thanks to a constant supply of babies which Mom produced from time to time. A weekly exchange of bread by Mom for packets of tea was then made and peace descended, but not for long.

FAMILY LIFE WITH DAD

Whilst awaiting his supper, with grim visage and beer-bloated bottom lip, Dad sat staring at the soles of my boots. I was not wearing them at the time but my discomfort was nonetheless acute. I was frequently on the receiving end of Dad's wrath due to cheekiness, when he would throw a hobnailed boot towards me, propelled by an underarm flick which he sometimes used. I would move my head slightly, with practised care, allowing the laces to brush my face. The missile continued on its way, crashing into the much-scarred Victorian sideboard – an heirloom from my paternal grandmother's family – and rested near a cake stand. I would give a groan of mortal standard to placate my father who, if cheated of the accustomed scream, may well have unleashed his overhead 'Yorker' which was unplayable and degrading to the long suffering sideboard. The dents in the doors of this mute victim bore witness to my agility and Dad's inaccuracy.

Friday evening was known to us as Dad's weekly boot inspection. These were required to show ten studs each, so on Thursday evening John and I had to furiously replace any missing studs in time for Friday's parade. The boots must never show any sole becoming worn and their immortality was further guaranteed by the provision of circular rubber screwed-on heels, which pivoted so that all areas would receive equal wear. Personally, I used them to stand on one leg and spin, preparatory to making a swift exit if the salvoes of footwear became barrages.

The explanation for this obsession probably stemmed from Dad's penurious childhood, when the ownership of a pair of boots was a coveted status symbol and the care of them was a daily necessity. Dad's alcohol-fuelled anger was deep-rooted, and his insistence that his two eldest sons maintain their boots in good order bordered on fanaticism. Unfortunately, he also insisted that we only wore boots - known as 'clod hoppers'. This caused me much anguish as, in 1944, I became the only boy from our council estate to go to Yardley Grammar School. My broad 'Brummie' accent, combined with my outlandish boots, caused much mirth amongst my peers, as did my school dinner tickets which were yellow instead of the usual red, indicating that I qualified for free meals. These humiliations have remained with me for life. But the boots regime effectively allowed my feet to develop normally and now, in my old age, I could make a fair crack of painting with my toes.

Our younger brother Fred had a new pair of boots, and Dad put in additional studs to make them last longer. Fred discovered that he could slide on the studs on the tarmac playground at school, so they wore down very quickly. One evening, Fred was taking off his boots and Dad picked them up, finding the studs very well worn down. Without any warning, he threw the boots at Fred and one hit his face, opening a gash across the brow of his eye, and blood started to pour down his face. He had to be taken to hospital to get the wound stitched up, following which an argument ensued between our parents, but Dad was adamant that it would teach Fred to take more care of his boots as 'money does not grow on trees'.

There were many times when John was in trouble, namely due to disagreeing with our parents, upsetting neighbours by tying cotton to door knockers, hiding behind hedges and pulling the cord. John used to make radio crystal sets and threaded the aerial up the stairs and into the loft, so our parents would catch their feet in the cable and trip, sometimes causing them to fall down the stairs.

John knew that he would often get a hiding from our father when he came home so he would stay hidden in the garden until everyone was in bed, often very late at night. Ronnie would then light a match or cigarette lighter to signal to John the coast was clear so he could climb the downpipe into the bedroom.

Our father tended to be very severe when doling out corporal punishment. John was always a rogue and frequently got into real trouble with the inevitable outcome. Both our parents were equally stubborn, and it wasn't uncommon for the dining room table to be left untouched for days on end because neither would give in and clear it. Mom had a terrifying habit of writing notes to leave for Dad on the mantelpiece, telling him what John and I had been up to, and we knew we would be severely walloped when he got back from the pub and we eventually crept out of hiding.

On one occasion John saw some radishes growing in the vegetable area next door and managed to push his arm through the hedge and pull out three radishes, which he then washed and ate. The neighbour called and told Dad that someone had pulled up some of his radishes. Subsequently, Dad asked if John was the culprit, which he admitted. Dad then cut a long piece of privet from the hedge and proceeded to bare Johns back and bottom, lashing him unmercifully until he bled; he was 13 years old. Our grandmother saw the state he was in and put ointment on the weals, while John tried desperately to hold back his sobs, but he was in agony, and the scars remained visible all his life. I tried to comfort him as much as I could as he had always looked out for me throughout our years together as evacuees.

Meal times at weekends were a virtual battleground, as any wrong doing would warrant a reprimand and a severe clip round the ear. On one occasion, when everyone sat around the table at Sunday lunch, John remarked that the meat was tough to eat. The next second he was flying through the air, as Dad had given him a huge punch across his face with the back of his hand which caused John to end up against the wall. He moved very fast towards the door before another enormous fist landed on his ear and he made it within a millisecond. This happened regularly as Dad always went to the local pub before Sunday lunch, and always insisted that John sat next to him.

For years, the atmosphere at home was terrible. John and I used to creep out of bed and listen at the top of the stairs to utter pandemonium, as our parents were having daily rows and upsets. Despite Mom working ceaselessly in a laundry, grocers' shops and as pub pianist, the rows were over lack of money, the amount of liquor consumed and accusations by Dad that Mom was too friendly with men. I have a painful memory, when aged five, of being pulled into one such argument by the ear, with Mom shouting at Dad that it proved I was his son for, like my siblings, behind it I have two little dimples.

One weekend was particularly violent, with items being thrown and hair being pulled, until Dad tried to leave by the front door, but Mom was too quick and shut the door violently, catching his leg and causing a huge cut down his shin almost eight inches long. The shouting and screaming got louder until Dad had to stem the bleeding with a towel and drive to the hospital. It was eventually stitched up but took many weeks to heal as he couldn't take time to rest.

Frequently rows at home were because Dad was such a jealous man and he resented Mom's popularity. She was an accomplished pianist and singer, who regularly gave musical evenings, playing and singing in local pubs where the customers' 'whip round' was depended upon. One evening Mom and Dad went to the Dog & Jacket pub in Kingsbury where there was a wedding celebration, and everyone had enjoyed Mom playing the piano. At midnight a crowd of inebriated people poured out and Mom stood by the car waiting for Dad to reverse from between two vehicles.

Suddenly there came a blood-curdling scream which had everyone transfixed in terror; Dad had run over Mom's foot! Dad stopped the car to discover what the problem was, but then reversed again over Mom's foot which made her screech even louder. With help the car was quickly removed, but the damage was done as she had three broken toes. Mom was taken to hospital, where they had to cut her shoes off, and her foot was in plaster for over a month – but Dad was in the doghouse for much longer than that. Mom was unable to play the piano for many weeks as she couldn't find the piano pedal due to her plastered foot.

*

John and I were inseparable and gained solace in each other's company, escaping the turmoil we lived in by creating our own daring and hazardous escapades, forming mutual respect and admiration and a bond that remained steadfast for the rest of our lives…

'Nickle Eck' and John, 1938

Eric and John, 2003

Illustrations by John Ashton

PART TWO

Childhood Mischief in Wartime Birmingham

1. RED LIGHT AHEAD

During our formative years when we lived with Mom's parents and other relatives, John continued to profoundly irritate his elders and was considered by our Auntie Elsie to be a 'little bleeder'.

John used to prowl around the house with a screwdriver, undoing the screws on the doorknobs so that anyone opening the door would end up with the handle in their hand with no way of opening the door. This lead to threats of caning, starvation, or being locked in the cellar. Grandad tried to catch John to give him a hiding, but he was much too quick and agile for him and would end up undoing the door knob from the inside of his bedroom so he couldn't be caught.

The final straw that broke the patience of every adult in the house was the two gallon tins of paint. Grandad had purchased red paint for floor tiles that had to be repainted every 2-3 years in the hallway, kitchen and living room. The paint was left behind the settee in the living room, but John decided he would do the job for Grandad, and enlisted my help. I was very reluctant as Grandad was a very formidable man, being six-foot-six with a raging temper when roused. However, I watched John as he pulled the two paint tins out and took them into the kitchen, using the end of a spoon to prise off the lids. Brimming with confidence he decided it would be quicker to spread the paint over the floor, which he did by tipping up both paint tins.

An enormous pool of red paint rapidly spread across the floor, under the cooker, the kitchen cabinets and cupboards. The paint was everywhere and John had overlooked that we had to walk across it to get outside, leaving red paint marks from our shoes all down the garden path. Very unsuccessfully, we tried to clean them off with paper and rags.

"This is going to take some explaining," I thought.

We were about to leave the garden when we heard a mighty roar coming from the kitchen, together with blasphemous comments and swear words, half of which we didn't understand. Eventually, Grandad hurled himself out of the kitchen running after us, wearing gumboots, but he slipped on the concrete path and fell with a crash, letting out unspeakable oaths.

We raced out of the back gate and hid, peeping over the wall until things quietened down. We then wandered up to the front door, where John was grabbed and given a right hiding by Dad. It took weeks to clear up the mess as the paint was very slow to dry.

This episode was the final straw; John and I left our grandparents' house in Small Heath a few weeks later with Mom and Dad, to begin our new life at 20 Dalston Road.

2. UNHOLY SMOKE!

The week did not start well. My elder brother John's imagination had been influenced by the latest 'Cowboys and Indians' epic at a Saturday morning matinee and he decided that we must practise throwing tomahawks.

"Why, John?" I demurred. "There aren't any Indians around here."

"That's what General Custer said," he replied, "and look what happened to him."

John's peroration lacked finesse but was, as usual, unanswerable.

"What about tomahawks?" I queried desperately, in an attempt to ward off imminent disaster.

"We've got a chopper," John triumphantly pointed out, squashing my hope for a long and tranquil life.

And so I became a Sioux Brave, armed with a blunt woodchopper which I was instructed to throw at our six-foot-high back gate. Time and again I hurled the chopper but it wouldn't stick in, being top-heavy and having the disadvantage of not being made by a Sioux warrior. I grew tired and offered the chopper to my brother brave.

"Just one more go," ordered John.

So I recharged my remaining puny muscles and feebly threw the chopper. It flew lazily through the air and met with our itinerant Potato Man, who sold potatoes from the back of his horse and cart and who chose that very moment to open the gate. Fortuitously the Potato Man was struck not by the blade but the shaft – which hit his chest with an interesting hollow sound.

The air was charged with silent reactions. The Potato Man rubbed his bruise and thought that his potatoes were not bad enough to warrant such a reception, John thought it an inconvenient moment to open the gate, and I thought of leaving the locality to summon the U.S. Cavalry. The Potato Man complained to Mom about us hooligans; Mom thumped our heads and bought five pounds of King Edwards.

John and I slunk off, hoping that the week would improve. It didn't.

Bonfire Night was approaching but we had no money for fireworks. John was irked, and John's 'irks' were dangerous - for me.

We made a few whirlies, our version of the Catherine Wheel, on a grand scale. For these we punctured holes in old tin cans, firstly filling them with compacted, moist earth to make it easier to knock in the nails to make the holes, and fixed handles of long, looped wire to the top.

The emptied cans were then filled with crumpled newspaper – preferably the 'News of the World' – and dry sticks. We then ignited them through a suitably large hole and whirled them around.

After a while the resultant draught produced a furnace-like heat and the cans glowed red, a very satisfying sight especially in a darkened room. "John's a great engineer," I thought admiringly.

After a few minutes we tired of this, and contemplated the eternal verities. Suddenly John's eyes shone with a familiar glint.

"IDEA!" he said.

My heart did its normal plummet and I sighed as I contemplated yet another cataclysmic event which would surely truncate my life on Earth.

John's fascination with pyrotechnics was kindled at an early age. Aunts, uncles and grandparents used to recount the great disaster at Coventry Road, Small Heath, where we lived when I was four. The house was lit by gas, and John was always fascinated by bonfires and forever gathering timber, cardboard, and paper which he lit in the garden. He was always dispatching me with a rolled-up newspaper for a light from the gas burners.

One day the main central chimney in our grandparents' Victorian three-storied house had caught fire, a routine experience in the days of coal fires, and the flames had become somewhat fierce.

The Fire Brigade was called with horses pulling the fire engine, and its spectacular arrival had inflamed my brother John's imagination; such colour and bustle, such ringing of bells, such unrolling of white walled hoses, such glamour. The firemen connected the long hoses to a large tank full of water and turned a huge wheel to pump the water up the chimney. They then pushed rods up the chimney to clear out as much soot as possible, following which they loaded up their equipment and departed.

John's young brain yearned for a repeat performance, so that after the chimney fire had been dowsed and quantities of tea consumed he was crestfallen. He lurked morosely and was inconsolable. He then had the first of his planet moving

IDEAS (again, John always thought in capital letters). He had decided that we should bring back the Fire Brigade; all that was needed was a fire.

John sent me into the cellar to bring up some kindling sticks. I happily obliged and, with the help of some old newspapers, we sat in front of the fire grate under the recently-quelled chimney fire, and coaxed dry sticks and newspaper into a welcoming glow. Placing a broad piece of newspaper over the grate John induced the flickering flames to a healthy roar and black, sooty smoke came out of the top and bottom of the chimney. We were both covered from head to toe with soot and resembled a pair of penguins, with only our eyes visible.

John and I welcomed the returning Fire Brigade with great enthusiasm and stood to attention with stern-faced salutes; they doused the fire, but the room was left in a terrible state. We were both dumped into the kitchen sink and scrubbed all over, but it took days for the soot to disappear completely. John had a hiding from Dad and also from Grandad, who threatened to whip him with a horse whip – but Dad prevented that.

There was a great deal of trouble after this show of independence; we were kept in for the rest of the week and punished by being separated. Meanwhile, the downstairs floors, walls and ceilings all had to be repainted.

John told me he was unfairly treated just because he had previously experimented with a red-hot poker, taken from the ever-glowing living room fire. With this he practised 'poker work' by laying it on work surfaces to observe the reaction of the material. Bakelite, he reported, smoked furiously but wouldn't burn, aluminium bent and sagged, electric wire burnt through and sparked – and all the lights went out. Iron was not affected, but wood satisfyingly singed, smoked and left an imprint. He loved making holes in newspapers when a small hole would expand into a larger one, surrounded by a glowing circle. Our Dad was observed to be unenthusiastic when he tried to read his newspaper after his return from the pub. Dad frowned frequently when his interest in an article was curtailed by a blackened hole, through which he would glower at us.

*

So, John's destructive capacities were re-kindled as he considered experimenting further.

"Gunpowder," he pronounced, elongating the three syllables into the equivalent of Henry V's speech on St. Crispin's Day.

"Wha'?" I managed (my Brummie accent had long abandoned ultimate 't's).

"We will invent gunpowder," said John, decidedly.

"Isn't it already invented?" I replied, in a vain attempt to stay alive.

"We will invent *a better* gunpowder," said John, squaring his jaw, his shoulders – and his conscience.

We sat and searched our minds for recipes, but could only come up with the mixture for stink bombs – sulphur and acid, preferably hydrochloric from old batteries. Fortunately we didn't know that this basic formula in quantity also produces poisonous gas, which John was quite capable of experimenting with on me and little friends, in an improvised test. But he didn't, so I'm still here.

At home we inspected an old Pears' Encyclopaedia and struck gold. Saltpetre was the essential ingredient for fireworks, fattened out with charcoal and sugar to make pretty fizzes and crackles.

We were ecstatic and pooled our meagre pennies to purchase the necessary saltpetre and charcoal from an old-fashioned dry-goods merchant in Yardley, where we did odd jobs on Saturday mornings. John then sent me into the chemist to buy sulphur 'as a secret ingredient'. Sulphur was then readily available and I was dispatched to make the purchase because of my innocent demeanour.

"Who would ever suspect you of making explosives?" asked John, rhetorically.

The Chemist looked at me benignly and leaned over the counter.

"And what do you want sulphur for little man?" he purred.

"Please Sir," I piped, suitably primed by John, "it's for soaking my dad's feet."

"Right you are young sir," the Chemist chuckled in a Dickensian manner, handing over the powder.

I rejoined John and we streaked off, intent on our preparation for war. We carefully mixed the ingredients in one of Mom's orange-coloured crock bowls with a wooden spoon (John suggested using a Runcible spoon but we didn't have one) and added a few match heads as detonators.

"Now, we pondered, what can we use as a casing?" John's ingenuity quickly galloped to the rescue.

"Nuts and bolts!" he shouted, and then added, "big ones, from the shelters."

He quickly explained that we would use two bolts, screwed either side of a large nut, and that our mixture would be poured into the space between the two. The nuts and bolts holding Anderson air-raid shelters together were huge and 'just-the-job'.

"But how are we going to get these nuts and bolts?" I foolishly enquired. John glared at me.

"Granite Swede," he snarled.

John never swore, but his colourful Arabic-type epithets were much admired. I thought he was being complimentary which he was, sometimes (about as frequently as the appearance of Haley's Comet). Apparently, 'Granite Swede' didn't mean a hard man from Scandinavia, but a thick-head from Dalston Road.

"You go and find a shelter in the garden of a house that's been evacuated or bombed out," he said, handing me an enormous spanner which came with our shelter kit, "and be quiet when you get back."

"Nobody notices you," he added with a final salvo.

"What a leader," I thought, as I crept off, carrying my conspicuous giant spanner over my shoulder. *"Hi ho, hi ho, it's off to work I go,"* I whistled, to fortify my wispy courage. I could have done with the comforting presence of six more dwarves, but no such luck.

I found a suitable Anderson shelter and started to unscrew the bolts, which were galvanised and therefore not rusty. It was not easy to go unnoticed, sitting on top of a corrugated sunken hut unscrewing bolts, but my overworked guardian angel somehow blanked me out.

My task completed, I shouldered the nuts and bolts in an old sack and headed for home. The sack swung from side to side, so I had to sway the opposite way to maintain equilibrium and I needed both hands to hold it. The long spanner was thrust down my shorts, causing me much pre-pubescent pain. Thus, I oscillated back home and dropped the swag at John's feet. I think he was surprised to see me again, as my approach was not, as planned, inconspicuous. However, the hardware was acceptable and we constructed the missiles.

John turned the nuts a few threads down on to the bolts and I carefully filled the resulting space with our mixture. He then gingerly screwed another bolt on top of each nut, and we were ready. We selected a flat concrete area in front of Dad's garage and prepared to smash the bolts down. I meekly suggested that John should have the honour of the first go. John gazed at me in disdain; he knew a cowardly poltroon when he saw one. He strode forward and hurled a bolt down.

Nothing happened; no explosion, no take-off - and no fizzles.

"No pressure," said John, taking a spanner and handing one to me.

"We have to tighten the bolts on to the gunpowder."

We increased the pressure by several more threads.

"Your turn," said John.

I stepped forward, quickly went through the Lord's Prayer, shut my eyes, and threw the firework down. Unfortunately I missed the flat surface and hit the slope in front of it.

A tremendous explosion ensued; the upper bolt took off and performed a perfect curve, arcing and spinning across the street and through the front bedroom window of the private house opposite. "That's going to take some explaining," I thought.

"Quick, fire the rest of them off," hissed John.

"Why," I asked timidly, but unhesitatingly complied and we mortared the surrounding area with satisfying exploding bolts.

"Fifth Columnists," replied John and, noting that I was struggling with this concept, he added, "and land mines."

I gave up and started to wonder who might come to my funeral.

"Fifth Columnists are like spies," John went on, "they lie low and sabotage everything after the war, and detonate land mines long after they've been dropped."

"Ah," I said gravely, "but what about the other four?"

John shrivelled me with a look.

"Just shurrup and tell everyone you meet what I've said," he instructed.

And so it was. I told everyone I met about Fifth Communists smashing windows and nobody queried my message. We were never identified as the culprits, although Mom suspected complicity and we got thumped anyway.

3. RODERICK'S BEER

Money in the pocket was hard to come by during the Second World War. Dad gave Mom a basic sufficiency to pay for rent, insurance policies (3d per week), electricity, gas, water, and soap, but left precious little for such luxuries as food and clothing.

Fortunately Mom was a superb cook, and fed her family handsomely on slow-cooked dishes from cheap off-cuts of meat and offal, befitting the daughter of a master butcher. But we dined often on what we later discovered to be 'Umble Pie'. How prophetic. It was therefore very important to find trickle sources of income to give our family purchasing power.

Mom was in great demand as a pub pianist, where she played splendidly by ear all the popular tunes of the day, her 'music' consisting of a list of song titles written on the back of cornflake packets.

Mom's performance was enhanced by a striking soprano voice. Towards the end of an evening's entertainment her rendition of *Just My Bill*, *Jealousy*, and *The Little Boy that Santa*

Claus Forgot engendered widespread anguish. These songs, Mom knew, would cause her paralytic patrons to drop tearstained silver sixpences into the passing hat, instead of the reluctant coppers dropped by the more hard-hearted.

We six siblings, four of whom were born between 1939 and 1946 – the result of Dad's contribution towards the War effort – had to earn our keep, and the results would be inspirational to emerging Third World countries. The usual exploit was to return empty bottles to shops and off-licences (known in those days as 'Outdoors') for 2d each – multiplied by the number of times we could climb over the back fence, retrieve more bottles and claim a further 2d *from a different shop!* Less cunning pilferers tried returning the bottles to the same shop; but what did they know? They didn't have the Machiavellian mind of my big brother John.

John was two years older than me and was, in reality, a young polymath with a questing brain full of ideas (or IDEAS – as they were always momentous) which often required experimentation on humans who were represented by me. I was small and meek, and would follow John into disaster after disaster: I did not expect to survive childhood.

John always explained his plans to me with logical panache, but I rarely understood. I always knew, however, that his plans were wondrously conceived and their birth would result in my incineration, poisoning, an explosion, or even death. He always had an answer to my squeaky objections and would thunderously cow me, by referring to my small stature containing a brain that was "No bigger than a sparrow's ankle."

My only defence, when I emerged from an experiment with blackened face and a limp, was to tell an enraged Mom, "John did it."

Carol singing was a very lucrative source of income but somewhat constrained by the necessity of confining it to the immediate period before Our Lord's birthday. I tried to sing in February but my efforts were poorly received and I reluctantly restricted my efforts to December. My personal slant on carol singing was to select as partner anyone who could not sing a note in tune, which would enhance my God-given high soprano voice which soared with heart-stopping purity as I sang *We Free Kings of Orion Tar*. I learned to wear ragged clothes, scuffed boots and a holey balaclava which, together with my haunted expression, caused blue-rinsed matrons in detached houses to press hot sixpences into my cold little hands.

My personal source of regular income derived from recycling wreaths from Yardley Cemetery. For a while I had a little job with a florist, who complained that flowers were relatively easy to buy but, as the War went on, it was almost impossible to purchase the woven wire bases for wreaths.

I offered to collect discarded wreaths from the nearby cemetery and he promised payment of threepence for each item. Foolish man! He thought that I would await the gathering of the tributes by the aged, creaky sexton, but I knew – from my observations in what was often my quiet playground – that grieving relatives rarely returned to the new graves and, if I discarded the flowers on to the graves in tasteful array, no-one would notice.

And thus it proved. I made several shillings a week until someone complained to the authorities that an elf was seen scampering around the graves with wreaths hanging from his neck. The resultant High Security alert frightened me off, and I haven't been back since.

So, when Dad said that I must fetch Roderick's beer every Sunday from an Outdoor nearby and deliver it to his house, I was interested in the payment. It never was a good idea to query anything Dad said unless you wanted the back of your head thumped, but I understood that I should collect two empty bottles and some money from Roderick's house at midday every Sunday, buy the beer and hand it over; 'Do you think you can manage that?'

Dad's sarcasm could be used as a weight on a fishing line. My mature six-year-old's reaction was to pretend that such remarks were genuine queries and I would respond by thanking him for his paternal concern and, with wide eyes, say that I would try very hard to carry out the mission. Such responses usually were uttered when I was near the back door, preferably open, to facilitate a hasty withdrawal to dodge the hobnailed boot carelessly tossed in my direction. The back door of our council house was liberally notched with deep indentations, which either bore silent evidence to my athleticism and extraordinarily quick reactions, or Dad's poor aim. I did ask about remuneration, but was fobbed off with an infuriating "It depends…"

So, every Sunday I went to Roderick's house on an errand which was handed down from brother to brother (or sister) for several years. I didn't know who he was, what his connection with Dad was, or any single detail of his life. I noticed that a grey female presence was often in the kitchen, which implied that he was normal, as most men had a grey presence in the kitchen on Sunday mornings cooking dinner. Not lunch; dinner was our word – like school dinners and dinner ladies.

'Roderick', never Mister or Sir or any salutation of any sort except the hard Brummie 'urgh' which preceded any sentence addressed to a grown-up. Thus: "Urgh! Can I go out?"; "Urgh! Can I use the clothes line to practise hanging my brothers?"; "Urgh! Why are you lying on the floor Dad?" – requiring a rapid exit closely followed by the hobnailed boot.

Roderick gave me money and two pop bottles (so-called as lemonade bottles had wired stoppers which, when first opened, went 'pop') and the order: "Two pints of Ansell's mild." This drink was brown, weak beer which, when consumed in oceanic quantities, turned men into menaces.

I ambled up the road, gazing in uncomprehending awe at the gardens of neat private semis, all of which had privet hedges and blue and white borders of 'Little Dorrit' and lobelia. Many had a monkey-puzzle or 'Golden Rain' tree.

The name *'Outdoor'* was adopted from Pubs for the sale of beer, cigarettes and Smith's crisps with the little blue paper twist of salt. Wine was not sold – the only one I knew of was *'Wincarnis'*. Youngsters as young as three or four were in the queue for beer; the only constraint offered to under-age customers was a sticky slip of paper stuck over the stopper. I collected my two pints, which was draught beer pulled by brightly polished Gaskell & Chambers beer engines into copper tun dishes. One pint was two pulls, and I watched as the stoppers were covered with the sticky paper tapes. I paid with the exact money so I didn't need to wait for change, and zoomed off to the nearest alley, where I quickly unstuck the tapes, which didn't stick very well to the beer-wet necks, and drank a couple of mouthfuls from each. This habit I acquired as a toddler during many boisterous parties at home, with Mom playing the piano amongst forests of bottled beer. It was my task to collect the empties for the precious 2d return, and store them away from likeminded children. Often the bottles were not quite empty, so I drank the dregs and slept well as a result. I swiftly became the youngest alcoholic in Birmingham.

Quickly hopping over a fence to an outside garden tap I topped up the depleted bottles with pure Birmingham Municipal water (all the way from the Elan Valley in Wales), replaced the tapes and ambled back to Roderick, who gave me a whole sixpence for my efforts. I often peeked through the kitchen door into their parlour, where I was astounded to see a bowl of fresh seasonal fruit, which no one ever ate. I knew I was outclassed.

My financial mission accomplished, I then returned home, being careful not to breathe fumes over my family.

4. GRANDAD'S HODGE

One Saturday morning in 1943, when we were living in Dalston Road, Birmingham, John became patriotic.

"We must help the War effort," he declared.

I looked for the nearest exit, which was an essential element in my survival plans whenever John had an 'IDEA!' (He thought in capital letters).

"Urgh, how?" I should have known better; I should have quietly left home and taken up botany.

John looked me up and down – which didn't take long.

"You're very small because you haven't got any brains," he concluded.

I knew that any retort would only confirm his diagnosis, so I kept quiet.

"We need to make something to sell to buy National Savings Certificates," John expounded.

"But what can we make?" I queried, timorously.

"Submarines," John replied.

"But won't that wake The Babby?" I asked.

"The Babby" was Fred, our first wartime brother, who weighed just over a massive 12lbs following a heroically long birth at home. The midwife commented each day of the long waiting period that the Babby was late. It seemed to me that it had probably forgotten the due date, not having a diary to refer to. Just after Fred was born, the midwife brought him downstairs, sat me in a chair, and carefully put him on my lap; it felt like being smothered by a large fragrant dog.

This, then, was the infant in his pram in the hallway, sleeping off several pints of full-cream milk with sugar added to match his gigantic appetite. Wartime babies qualified for extra rations which John and I helped to consume. John said that Fred couldn't eat meat or bread, so we were helping him out by eating for him; I hope he was grateful for our gesture as in adult life he became a JP with an MBE.

John glared at me again, so that my small stature shrank even more, and continued.

"Toy submarines – you Granite Swede; we will make a mould out of Plaster-of-Paris and fill it with molten lead," he explained, as if to a child, and triumphantly produced one of our few toys - a small metal submarine which had a flat bottom.

Plaster-of-Paris was well known and often used to reinforce makeshift splints at First Aid depots during enemy bombing raids. We could easily acquire some from these unguarded First Aid centres. Who'd ever pinch items to be used for the injured? We would – and did! John explained that most of it was wasted anyway, as it was broken off when the casualties reached hospital.

Lead was a different matter. I wisely didn't ask about

obtaining this material, as I had visions of crawling over the church roof hauling off pieces of guttering – pretending to be a gargoyle if anyone noticed me.

"Idea!" John said, ominously.

"Oh, no!" I wailed, racing to the kitchen door.

But John was too quick for me. He dragged me back and grabbed me firmly by the back of the neck as he stared into my eyes like a giant snake, while I awaited the bite of his forked tongue.

"Tennis," he said.

I relaxed. "That's alright," I thought. John released my head.

"It's a game," I said.

"Not the game, boiled brain," John thundered, "the line markings."

Very confused, but willingly, I followed John as he collected a claw hammer from Dad's toolbox and strode to a nearby park, which had a semi-derelict tennis court as most of the players were serving in the Armed Forces. I had the job of stripping the lead as I was small enough to squeeze through the rotting fence. We surveyed the scene, John pointed to the old markings and, sure enough, they consisted of thin strips of lead. He handed me the hammer and told me to strip up a yard or so of the base line, while he kept watch.

"Won't they miss it?" I asked nervously.

"They probably did when it was there," said John, enigmatically. "Now shurrup and yank."

I pulled up a section and we carried the weighty piece home. John cut several chunks off with a chisel and put them into a cast iron pot with a lip, originally used for melting wood glue in the garage.

We returned to the kitchen, where we mixed the plaster in a tin and pressed the toy submarine upside down into it.

While waiting for the plaster to set, we put the pot of lead on to the largest burner on the stove to melt, which it soon did – giving off great clouds of smoking fumes. We hurriedly opened the kitchen door and windows, and turned the burner down to 'simmer'. The house would not be habitable for several days, but that's a different story.

We then pulled the submarine out of its container and revealed a perfect mould. The plaster appeared hard and set, so we placed it on the wooden draining board and carefully carried over the pot of molten lead with Mom's large tongs, used for extracting clothes from our copper boiler.

John slowly lowered the pot on to the draining board, where it burned a neat circle and, at arm's length, gently tipped it to cascade the molten metal into the mould. That caused the next disaster.

What we had overlooked was the fact that, although the plaster was set, it wasn't dry. (We discovered later from a library book that plaster should be very, very dry, otherwise the hot lead would produce steam.) Clouds of steam enveloped us and the mould spat out dozens of perfectly formed lead shot into the ceiling. Miraculously we weren't hurt, although the condensing steam around our heads was somewhat uncomfortable. We laughed at first, then realized we had to clean up the walls, floor and cooker, which took us about two hours – but still left marks where paint was missing.

Worse was to come; our Grandad appeared at the kitchen door. He inhaled, coughed, and also spat into the back yard.

"What're you doing lads?" he enquired.

"Making submarines Grandad," I answered.

"Ah well," he said, "ask a silly question…"

He leaned over the hot lead pot and sniffed the contents. The fumes would have felled a bison, but Grandad seemed to enjoy them. He glanced at the ceiling, where cooling lead shot pinged down, intermittently.

"Tried to escape did it?" he smiled at us indulgently. "Never mind, I've brought you some real food."

This struck terror in my pounding heart. Grandad, a master butcher – who later opened a new butchery in Birmingham's Bull Ring – brooked no argument. He was a great bear of a man with a waxed moustache, winged collar, waistcoat, pocket watch, and *Albert* chain. He smelled gloriously of tobacco and snuff. The snuff was so fierce that a small pinch, once given to me to cure a sniffly cold, very nearly dispatched me. When I inhaled it my innards stopped working, my brain boiled and my belly churned – loudly. Only some mighty buttock-clenching prevented a shameful disaster. The snuff cured the sniffle and I could swear I could hear better afterwards.

When I stayed with Grandad (I was his favourite grandson out of a collection of about a hundred or so) he would place food in front of me that had been discarded from the meat market where he worked, and would have been avoided by hovering vultures. When I hesitantly asked what it was he would reply,

"It's good for you, gerrit down yer."

It wasn't a question of 'gerrying it down' me – it was keeping it down that troubled me. Withal, Grandad was a kind and jovial man who knew that meat was scarce and did his best to help. John and I would wait for Grandad to bring home meat, sausages and bacon every month or so in a horse-driven *Governess* cart.

He produced a bloodstained paper package.

"This is hodge," he said.

"Hodge?" we chorused suspiciously. "What's that, Grandad?"

"Pig's guts," he explained, "liver, kidneys, brains all wrapped in a stomach lining; it needs long, slow cooking."

He took a large saucepan off its hook, half-filled it with

water and placed the hodge in it (after removing most of the paper bag), added a huge chunk of salt broken off a block and lit the burner. A vile stench soon filled the kitchen and blended with the lead fumes. I didn't think I'd make it to the kitchen door. John stopped breathing in for the duration and went a funny colour.

Grandad had omitted to wash out the pig's last supper from its guts and the resultant fermenting contents added piquancy to the fricasse. He turned down the heat so that only an occasional grey bubble escaped the clutch of the goo, and prepared to depart.

"Don't forget – long, slow cooking," he instructed, and strode away with a final thrust, "tell your Mom what it is."

I didn't think that Mom would need to be told, as the life-threatening fumes could be discerned at the end of the street.

John and I stared at each other through the vile vapour.

"What shall we do?" I quavered. "I can't eat that."

"Stop moaning and shurrup," said John, "I'm thinking." His great brain sparked and crackled, "IDEA!" he said.

I was too weak through lack of oxygen to run, but I feared that my end was nigh.

"Dig for victory!" John shouted, like an animated poster.

"Wha'?" I gasped; my own contributions to the discussions were always minimal.

"We'll bury it, you crumpled skull – in the garden. Follow me, and bring a spade."

He grabbed the saucepan and marched into the front garden – a wilderness of tired weeds – with me bringing up the rear of the cortege with a spade on my shoulder and hope in my heart.

"Dig," said John, pointing to an earthy space.

I moved up-wind of the corpse and dug as quickly as I could.

"Faster," hissed John through tight lips and purple visage, "I can't stand the smell much longer."

I redoubled my burrowing and soon we had a shallow grave. John dumped the hodge and its accompanying sauce into its resting-place, filled in the hole and jumped on it. The interment of the hodge was without ceremony, although I did pray that it wouldn't grow.

We returned to the house, cleaned the saucepan and threw the spade into the back yard. I stared at the ring burn on the draining board and the remaining fragments of lead shot sticking to the ceiling. "This is going to take some explaining," I thought.

John wafted the fumes through the windows and doors with a towel and I wandered outside to breathe fresh air. Peace descended – but not for long.

As I gazed around I suddenly spotted a familiar tall figure approaching. I gasped and raced back into the kitchen.

"It's Grandad," I yelled to John, "he's coming back – he'll want to inspect the cooking!"

We were nonplussed – but only momentarily.

"We'll dig it up and re-cook it," said a wild-eyed John. "Quick – you act as decoy."

"Who's he?" I asked, not unreasonably.

"A decoy, you lampwick. A distraction – go and delay him."

John shoved me out of the door and made a speedy exit to fetch the spade and perform the exhumation.

Delaying Grandad in full stride was no easy task and, as his six-foot-six inch frame approached, I girded my loins and took on the mantle of David. Remembering that Grandad was very fond of me I rushed towards him and unleashed my sling-shot.

"I want to come-upper," I said, holding my arms up to him.

Grandad stopped and, beaming with delight, stooped and hoisted me on to his shoulders. 'Come-upper' was my childish phrase for him to pick me up when I was little. The view to my infant gaze was spectacular; the only drawback was that Grandad sometimes forgot to duck when passing through a doorway and I would be left hanging for a while, spread across the upper door frame. I became adept at clinging to the picture rails whilst my little legs were jammed against the upright doorframes. Grandad would return to find me.

"Ah! That's where you've been hiding," he would chuckle. Grown-ups always repeated the same joke, and laughed in an unseemly manner at their own wit.

As Grandad carried me nearer the garden I could see John acting like a demented mole, throwing up soil and hodge gravy. He needed another few minutes, so I threw my remaining shot.

"I want some suck, please." Grandad halted and put me down. 'Suck' was his word for boiled sweets, and he always carried a 'bag of suck' for his grandchildren.

He searched in his pockets and produced the bag of sweets. I selected one with the fewest tobacco shreds and snuff granules attached, and quickly sucked and salivated. The trick, much to Grandad's amusement, was to collect as much saliva as you could with the first suck, and spit it out whilst retaining the sweet behind your front teeth.

Grandad was a renowned and accurate spitter, and it was rumoured that he could douse a small fire at ten yards. In those days I often thought that Grandad could have given an exhibition in a fairground – next to the Fire Eater, where he could extinguish the flame with his mighty mucus.

John, by this time had disappeared back into the house, where he swilled off the hodge, replaced it in the saucepan with more salt and (a touch of genius) filled the pan with water from the hot tap, added his own ingredient, turned up the gas ring and was ready.

Grandad and I arrived and Grandad gravely inspected the brew, smelt it, gave it a stir and had a taste. He chewed several bits of clinging grit with a thoughtful look, cleared his throat, coughed, and spat out of the window. John and I ducked but, fortunately, it was open. Any passing duck would not have survived.

Grandad expressed his satisfaction and off he went, with a cheery wave and a wish that we should enjoy our dinner.

"You did it! You did it!" I crowed. "But where did you get that coloured water?"

"Gravy browning," said John airily, as we consigned the drained hodge to the dustbin suitably wrapped in the 'News of the World'.

I stared at John in stupefied admiration.

"You're great," I said.

"And you're an idiot," John said kindly.

"No I'm not," I said, having the last word for once, "I'm a decoy."

5. WINTER SPORTS

The clothesline was an essential part of our childhood and our education would have been poorer without its myriad uses, including trussing, so it was no great surprise when one bleak Saturday morning in December, my elder brother John approached me, carrying the line with an innocent expression – which on his face made Svengali look benign.

"If you were convicted of murder they would hang you," he confided in a terrifyingly friendly tone.

"They wouldn't," I quavered, "I haven't killed anybody."

"Yet," said John, "and I did say *if*."

"But…" I tried.

"Shurrup and listen," said John. "You can cheat the hangman," he whispered, "if you strengthen your neck muscles."

He went on to explain that he would wrap one end of the clothesline round the overhead bar across the top of our 6 foot high back gate and the other end around my neck, leaving me just able to stand underneath with my feet on the ground. I would then practise taking my weight, using my neck muscles by alternatively standing on my toes and crouching down.

"You don't weigh much," John observed, "and you'll soon get the hang of it."

So the line was fixed and I tried the exercise, tentatively. As the line was loosely wrapped under my chin it was, in fact, possible to take my weight using my hands on the line above my head, as well as my neck muscles.

I gained confidence and kept my feet off the ground, while a cold wind swung me from side to side.

Mom chose this moment to march up the garden path. She glanced up in the twilight to see her second son hanging from the gate bar, swinging silently gibbet-fashion, while her first-born stood and watched impassively.

Mom's wail of anguish was heard in the Bull Ring in Birmingham City Centre and, for all I know, in Pamplona.

"What in God's name are you doing?" she shrieked.

"John's teaching me to cheat the hangman," I replied, chokingly.

That is when I learned that telling the truth is occasionally misconstrued. Although John was walloped for setting up the execution I was also walloped for allowing it to happen, or perhaps I was walloped because I was safe and Mom was afraid that she had lost me – as fond parents often do after an errant child is found.

Our punishment continued when we were given buckets, forks and shovels and dispatched to the coalmines down at the canal wharves nearby. Domestic coal was always in short supply and was a vital commodity in most homes.

This activity was peculiar to our area, and was created by the

46

action of giant machines dredging the canal near the coal wharves to keep the coal barges moving, to supply the desperately needed coal for homes and industry. The resultant dumps at the sides of the wharves were sticky, evil-smelling swamps, which contained 'black gold', namely lumps of coal.

Hitherto, John and I had gathered winter fuel by hurling abuse and stones from the canal bank at passing coal barges (never 'narrow boats'; such a term is modern pretentiousness). The Bargees would respond with their own untranslatable abuse and hurl lumps of coal at us, which we gleefully collected – under fire, so to speak.

But the Dump Mines were a different scuttle. The weather was bad, Siberian cold with gusts of snow, and a wasted landscape swarmed with children and old men, digging and scraping for the precious nuggets of coal. The children could only tackle the hard surface, which they broke with hammers to reach the viscous ooze beneath. They would then probe with their forks like blackened Swiss rescue teams searching a crevasse. If the tines of the forks hit an obstruction, it was hurriedly dug out and dropped into a well guarded bucket – for marauding coal rustlers were a constant threat, and claim jumpers were not unknown.

Men dug deep holes, which were dangerous, but they gathered much more – and larger lumps. At the end of their shift they would invariably collapse the entrance to their mines, in true working men's Christian tradition, before carrying home their spoils, bless them.

John and I joined in and found a likely spot. We dug and scraped for a while and our bodies warmed a little with the effort, but our hands froze into claws, which mercifully became numb.

John noticed a group of children nearby, who were doing quite well, and told me to go over and boast about the rich vein, which we had found.

"But we haven't," I said plaintively, "and if I tell them that we have, they'll come across and take it over."

John looked at me pityingly, "Precisely, my dear Watson." How John loved his Sherlock Holmes.

"But…" I tried again.

"Shurrup and do what I said." John won the argument with his usual aplomb.

So I wandered off and boasted and bragged to great effect, adding, at John's suggestion, that we weren't going to share with anyone. That did the trick. Noticing that there were only two of us they marched across to our patch pushed us off and began to dig furiously; greed had got to them.

I prepared to go home with our meagre load.

"Where are you going, Nickle Eck?" (Derived from 'Little Eric' one of my family's pet names for me).

"Home," I replied, dispiritedly.

"No we're not," said John, with shining face and hideous grin. He marched over to the vacated diggings of our usurpers where we dug lots of lumps, well before our victims had realised, alas, that our previous plot was barren.

On our way out of the mines with our precious cargo, I wistfully noticed several children sliding down slopes on improvised wooden sledges, and wished aloud that we could make a sledge and join in. John came to an abrupt halt. His eyes glowed with a familiar glint, "IDEA!" he said.

My heart sank, my cold, purple lips tried to say, "Oh, no," and I looked around for a suitable bolthole. John's ideas always worked, but the participants were often maimed or went missing.

"Tell as many kids as you can to gather on the canal tow path tomorrow (Sunday) morning for the greatest sledge ride of their lives," he instructed authoritatively.

I zoomed around and passed on the message, suitably embellished with details of the number of reindeer involved. By the time I was seven I was an angelic-faced consummate liar.

John was enigmatic about his plans but I could tell that his giant brain boiled with masterly planning for the event.

Six inches of snow fell that night, and the morning was very cold. We therefore dressed in many layers of clothes and crowned ourselves with our most precious items – Balaclavas. These had been knitted by our Gran, Dad's mother, who lived with us. Gran spent most of her time unravelling old woollies and then knitting huge socks for 'our lads at The Front'. (As she had lost a son in the First World War she thought that our lads were still fighting the Hun on the Somme.) Gran also knitted comforters, which were strangely shaped and gave no clue as to which portion they would comfort.

Thus, our Balaclavas kept us warm but were constructed out of many differently coloured skeins of wool, so we looked distinctly alien in the white landscape.

Arriving at the canal John outlined his plan. The assembled volunteers were led to a pile of 'spare' corrugated iron sheets at the wharf, used in the construction of air raid shelters.

"There is our sledge," said John, pointing to one of the roofing sheets which curved at one end resembling a huge sledge. In military fashion John ordered us to carry this to the top of the steep bridle path, used by the barge horses to cross over to the other side of a bridge which had no towpath.

After much slipping and struggling the curved sheet was placed at the top of the path, which was lined with a post and rail fence. Here John halted the work and, using his clipped accent borrowed from officers in war films, he issued his battle plan.

"Construct a camber," he said, with Napoleonic certainty.

"Wha'? Wha'? Wha'?" we chorused, staring at him with total incomprehension.

John relented a little. "As you will have observed, there is a bend in the path," he barked. We hadn't – but there was.

"So," John continued, "you will all roll big snowballs down the banks and pack them on one side of the bend to form a sloped camber, so that the sledge will tilt and slide round. GO!"

Dozens of children scattered and began rolling great balls of new, soft snow down to the bend. Some became too big and rolled on inexorably, flattening slow-moving toddlers in their path. Perhaps some were consumed and became part of the balls; I don't know. Nobody ever counted.

John and I, meanwhile, had inspected the thickness of the ice covering the canal. John, of course, allowed me to walk on to the ice to test its thickness.

"Why me?" I quavered.

"You don't weigh much," said John.

There seemed to be a flaw in his reasoning but I was too terrified to work it out and dutifully slithered out on to the floe. It didn't break and I skidded back to safety.

John nodded but didn't offer any commendation, nor was there any noticeable welcoming party.

We rejoined the rolling snowballers and gathered round the sledge, after John had inspected the new camber.

"Bob-sledging is safe," he proclaimed. After this prevarication I expected a divine thunderbolt to strike him – but the Gods were busy elsewhere.

"Now," said John importantly, "the older racers will push the front part and jump on when we start moving. You younger kids sit at the rear now, before we start. Wait for the word of command," he concluded.

We took our places; John and me at the front leaning against the iron curve and the little ones at the back, staring wild-eyed with excitement.

John addressed the multitude; he probably expected me to distribute loaves and fishes, but barked, "Now for the ride of your lives!" "Or your last one," I thought.

"Now – PUSH…"

We moved slowly off down the path, watched by a small crowd of onlookers on the bridge. There were no ambulances or fire engines lined up, so I committed my soul to everlasting peace and jumped on with everyone else.

At first all went well, as we sailed sedately down the slope, then our speed increased as we approached the inclining bend. The iron ship rocked and magically tilted as it soared round the bend, discarding several small passengers on its centrifugal journey.

On we plunged at an ever-increasing rate down the steepest slope. Breathing became difficult as the freezing air forced its way into our orifices. This was living – for a while at least. The landscape sped past and the fence became a blur as we accelerated towards the towpath. I looked across at John with my special 'please-stop-this-experiment-and-let-me-go-home' look, but he disdained to react to my plea and we stormed on.

We jounced across the towpath and took off over the ice. In Einstein-pleasing fashion time slowed down; "This is nice," I thought, as we flew through the air. "What a leader John is."

We touched down with some force and the ice could be heard cracking, but our speed was such that we rushed on regardless, heading for the opposite bank. Being well accustomed to John's experiments I adopted my usual recovery position, re-forming myself as a foetus.

Our massive iron-clad sledge hit the towpath with a terrific bang, stopped abruptly. It dipped its head into mushy ice at the foot of the bank and flipped its tail up like a harpooned whale. This action crushed the front passengers into a bruised ball, but catapulted the tots at the rear into the air, increasing their original velocity. In the ensuing time warp I uncurled and looked up to see the tots fly overhead in perfect formation like little Spitfires. They landed safely in snowdrifts, brushed themselves down and struggled up the bank towards home to brag about their adventure to their moms – but omitting the final 'wizard prang'.

John and I, together with the other survivors at the front, scrambled out of our slowly sinking craft and limped away.

But we held our bruised heads high; we were now experienced bob-sledgers and the *Cresta Run* seemed a possibility.

All was peaceful – for a while...

6. THE DALSTON ROAD IRREGULARS

My elder brother John and I were voracious readers from a very early age – four years in my case – amply provided for by our splendid local library, backed up with adverts on the back of bus tickets and the contents lists and recipes on sauce bottles (fricasse was called 'frick-arse' with much merriment). Our love of reading was not at first through any literary urge but as a result of our unremitting curiosity, unassuaged to this day, and of course the library was quiet and warm. These latter bonuses were magical and rarely enjoyed at home.

We had no guidance concerning suitable authors or subjects, so we decided to start by reading one author's books at a time, working through the alphabet. Thus, I read Boccaccio, Samuel Butler, Richmal Crompton, Charles Darwin, and so on. Some books were incomprehensible, some were interesting and some were a delight. John and I became familiar with Just William, King Solomon's Mines and the immortal Sherlock Holmes in our early reading, as these stories occurred early in the alphabet. Our conversations sometimes became a secret communication code unrelated to *The Beano* and *The Dandy*.

'In the Country of the Blind the one-eyed man is King' goes the old saying, but one of our eyes was often closed by the fists of the jeering bullies who objected to our being different. We therefore hid our little learning – John became taciturn and stern; I became a comic actor and buffoon; I still am.

This knowledge became useful when the neighbourhood decided our house had quite a large front garden on a corner site, well suited to a bonfire, but we had no fuel.

John and I were inconsolable. We wandered down to 'the Cut', as the nearby Grand Union Canal was known, whose overgrown banks of weeds and shrubs offered little solace. But then deliverance came: we spotted a fallen fir tree, blown over in recent gales, which lay with its roots pointing up the bank while its twiggy head, covered in dying needles, was obviously ideal bonfire material. Oh joy! Oh joy! – But then my natural Doubting Thomas alter ego took over.

"It's too big," I said. "How do we get it home?"

John pondered, an awesome sight; then his face lit up.

"IDEA!" he said.

My little heart plummeted to my ankles. John's ideas bordered on genius but the practical details always contained the promise of mayhem and brotherly destruction.

John's eyes glinted.

"The Baker Street Irregulars – Sherlock Holmes," he intoned, with the air of a renowned scholar.

I was, as usual, somewhat taken aback.

"We live in Dalston Road and you're not Sherlock Holmes," I pointed out, diffidently.

I was about to add that I was unqualified to act as Dr.

Watson, when John interrupted:

"I'm borrowing the idea," he said.

"Sherlock gathered local urchins to carry out some of his investigations and called them 'The Baker Street Irregulars', we will do the same and call them 'The Dalston Road Irregulars'."

"What's an urchin and what do they do?" I asked, trying to postpone disaster.

"Urchins," replied John, "are poor kids who will do anything for a reward – which in this case will be an invitation to our bonfire and, perhaps, a baked potato. So shurrup and listen…"

"They will drag the tree up the bank, over the road at the top and up the street to our bonfire." He trumpeted, triumphantly.

In John's mind, the Great Fire of Dalston Road was already lit and natives danced around the pyre, complete with loin cloths and war cries, while some poor wretch tied to a stake – probably me – slowly roasted.

So, we gathered our Irregulars together, mainly seven or eight-year-olds with a sprinkling of toddler camp followers, and marched off in irregular order led by John, carrying our all-important clothesline to aid the tugging. I brought up the rear like a sheep dog, rounding up the stragglers.

At the canal bank we surrounded the tree and everyone grasped a branch. The toddlers were placed inside the canopy and told to brace their backs under a limb. Several immature voices complained that they couldn't see, were being pricked by needles and wanted to go home.

"If we don't get this tree home you'll never see anyone again," thundered John.

The mutiny subsided, apart from a few squeaks – which John promised to silence with the lash or by walking the plank.

The clothesline, from which we had thoughtfully removed the damp garments and pegs at home, was tied around the stump and anchored around John and me. We were ready; silence surrounded us.

"On the word of command," said John, using the clipped tone used in war films, "you will heave - upwards."

He took a deep breath and bawled, "MUSH!"

"Mush?" I queried, hesitantly.

"It's what the Eskimos shout at their dogs pulling their sledges," hissed John. "Now, shurrup and pull."

Miraculously the giant tree began to move up the bank. Inch by inch it seemed to claw itself upwards as the huskies and their pups heaved and pushed their collective power against the branches.

When the top of the bank was reached, the root ball of our arboreal offering at first jutted up free, then gravity took over and it levelled out. This caused some consternation in the canopy. The toddlers suddenly found themselves airborne, clinging to their branches as the ground inexplicably fell away. Their little legs kept furiously moving in space, like frantic ducks on a pond suddenly deprived of water. They were too breathless to scream and only managed muling noises. John probably thought that building pyramids was similar to this and that casualties must be expected.

The pavement and gutter were crossed and the jouncing juggernaut faced the Red Sea of the main outer-circle road between us and home. We couldn't go sideways or backwards, nor could we stop as we would not be able to start again. Traffic was mercifully light. John shouted his cry of 'mush' and encouraged the (by now hidden) urchins to shout in unison of our common purpose. I said little, as by now my lungs had ceased their natural task.

We set off, and were rewarded by the goodly God of Firewood with a gap in the traffic. The road parted and we moved on majestically – with but one mishap. A laden trolleybus hove into view and screeched to a halt. The slack-jawed, stupefied driver saw two small boys pulling a large tree, complete with rootball, with a clothesline and no visible help.

The leader was shouting, "Mush! Mush!"

The tree was answering, "Bon-fire! Bon-fire!"

It was not recorded what the passengers thought, but many would attend Church on Sunday and promise to lay-off excessive alcohol for a few days – or hours.

The tree moved on past endless semi-detached houses, whose lace curtains twitched in sequence as it dragged itself past towards its spectacular doom.

Arriving home, John directed us through the privet hedge surrounding our garden, as the remnants of our gateway was too narrow, and we came to a lurching halt at the bonfire site. The exhausted irregular urchins were winkled free and laid out. Tea and biscuits were deserved but not available that particular Saturday, so pop bottles of water were distributed to the survivors and sprinkled over recumbent tots.

We all set to the task of demolishing the tree with borrowed saws and choppers, occasionally loading an upright branch with a dozen or so helpers until it cracked. The bonfire grew and grew until finally it was ready. We regarded the immense pile with exhausted pride, but dusk was gathering and it was time for the festival to commence. The question was – how were we to light the fire?

"Paraffin," said John, a man of few words and each of them ominous.

Paraffin was extensively used at the time for heaters and lamps, so I scuttled indoors to the bogey hole (the cupboard under the stairs) and returned with two pints. John poured it over the wood.

"Matches," ordered John.

I scuttled back indoors, returned, and proffered the firesticks to the Chief.

We all leaned towards the heap. John dropped the flame into a nest of dried leaves – and nothing happened.

"Newspaper," said John.

I repeated my well-rehearsed act and returned with an old '*News of the World*' (which Dad took for the sports news – or so he said). John crumpled it up and placed it at the bottom amongst the leaves. We crowded round and breathed in the balmy summer air, liberally mixed with paraffin fumes.

John struck the match, applied it to the redundant newspaper, and the whole pile went WHUMP, bursting into wonderful flames. We had done it – a bonfire of our own!

We gazed in wide-eyed awe for a few minutes, and then edged away from the privet hedge which was also burning well after ignition by the furnace-heat of the fir tree, aided by bursts of flame from super-heated resin. We distributed our whirlies, which were a great success and added to the spreading inferno as we whirled the flaming tin cans into the air to land in other hedges – we knew not where.

We happily gazed at the reflected glow in the sky and heard with mounting excitement the bells of the approaching Fire Brigade – the leading engine driven by Uncle Alf, (who served with distinction as a driver with the Auxiliary Fire Service during the Blitz) frantically speeding towards the conflagration at his sister's home. "This is going to take some explaining," I thought.

I looked round and saw the happy little blackened faces, shining in the blazing light. And yes, amongst the smiles and grins I could see that John was correct with his Sherlock Holmes reference; many of their teeth were distinctly irregular.

7. BREAD PUDDING

Mom's bread pudding was famous throughout the Birmingham council estate where we lived during the late-thirties and the Second World War. The pudding, which was always eaten cold on Saturdays, was made mainly from stale bread, water, some currants, a small amount of sugar and a pinch of cinnamon. The secret of its success was in the baking, of which Mom was an expert. Its consistency was firm, yet yielding like cheddar cheese, and the edges – Oh, the edges! – were dark brown and crisp. The slices bordered by the edge were fought over by dozens of neighbouring children, who gathered for a piece.

My elder brother John and I had first pick, and we were inclined to Lord it over the unseemly 'tableau vivant' outside by throwing pieces of pudding into the air above the throng, to enjoy the manic scramble of desperate kids. One boy, whose little brother was being trampled underfoot, stood on him to gain extra height, the standee repeating the often heard mantra "Fair shares, fair shares, fair shares", until his little lungs collapsed under the weight of his big brother.

One Saturday, Mom had to leave early for her job in a Laundry, so John and I decided to help her by making the bread pudding as a surprise: prophetic words. The build-up was easy, lots of stale bread, a few currants and water. But how much water?

"It doesn't really matter," said John. "If there isn't enough we add some; if there's too much we can squeeze it out."

So we stirred the mixture in the large brown crock bowl with plenty of water. After a while we stopped to examine it; we took handfuls and squeezed them, then stared at each other as it dawned on us that we had created a thick bread soup containing what looked like mouse droppings. We had to find a method of squeezing the water out, leaving a mache of bread mix to bake. But how?

"Idea!" said John.

He was the only person I ever met who said 'idea' like that. I could virtually see the cartoon balloon above his head reading 'IDEA!' My little six-year-old heart sank, my jaw clenched and little hairs all over began to stand on end as the adrenaline flowed. I knew that John's ideas always contained a grain of genius which mostly resulted in anguish, torment and raised bumps on the back of my head from parental thumps or hobnailed boots flung at my rapidly departing figure.

This time, however, the omens were good. The idea seemed soundly based and I could always blame John if anything went wrong. John explained that we should tip the mixture into a cloth and guide the ends of the cloth into the kitchen mangle, turn the handle slowly and 'Hey Presto!' the excess moisture would seep through the cloth into a waiting bucket, the residue being left in perfect condition for baking.

We set to and erected the mangle. It consisted of a worktop which, when raised, revealed the two mangle rollers connected to a large handle. We then had an inspiration, a pillowcase! Of course – just the job.

A pillowcase was fetched from the airing cupboard and duly filled with our mixture. The open end was carefully folded over and placed between the rollers, the handle turned to take up the slack, and we were ready.

"You first," said John.

So I bent my puny frame to turning the handle, but when the bulk of the mix reached the rollers all motion ceased.

"Harder – push harder," urged John, "imagine you're a galley slave with an oar," he roared, encouragingly.

"I don't want to be a galley sl–" I whimpered.

"Shurrup and push," said John.

So I strained and pushed and a few tiny beads of moisture oozed through the pillowcase.

I was shoved out of the way for being useless and John took the helm or, rather, the handle. He pushed and strained as I stood in front of the mangle watching the perspiration coming through the cloth and shouted.

"It's working, it's working!"

John put his feet against the adjacent wall and gave a Herculean heave. That did it. The pillowcase split and several pounds of pressurised bread soup burst forth and covered everything in its remorseless path, including me.

As the tornado of bread soup sped over and past me, I was encased from head to foot. My ears offered some resistance and formed two drifts, which cut off all sound. I had automatically closed my eyes when the pillowcase exploded, but my mouth was open (it often was) and it filled up, as did my nostrils.

Bizarrely, my upper torso was silhouetted on the wall behind me, body outlined as in an American murder investigation. John gazed at his transmogrified little brother, whose face was a blob, with small globes either side and two green eyes which gave out a thousand-yard stare and from which two warm tears formed tracks down the breaded nursery slopes of his cheeks. Overall I resembled a roughcast cherub.

John began to laugh, maniacally. I could not hear him but knew that his developing love of mayhem – particularly to others – was taking over. He doubled up, stamped his feet and danced like an Apache Brave round the mangle, whose twin rollers appeared to me to be grinning at my discomfiture.

After an unseemly long time John stopped laughing; a gleam came to his eyes and a stern look to his visage. I knew what was coming:

"Idea," he mouthed at me.

My heart, which was hovering near the quarry tiles of the kitchen floor, could drop no further. My adrenaline was spent and I was unable to orally object as I frantically tried to swallow a week's supply of carbohydrate.

John's plan, as ever touched by genius, was that as there wasn't time to wipe up the mess he would clean the gas rings on top of the stove and light them, then he would light the oven and leave the door open which would quickly dry the bread soup in situ; all we then had to do was strip it off the walls and nobody would be any the wiser.

I was ordered to the bathroom to clean myself. I misheard his instructions about my clothes, but John bent close to me, moved one of the bread drifts from an ear and bawled "Bath, bath, bath!" I heard that and oozed off, leaving a trail up the linoleum-covered stairs, which looked like the track of a ruminant with stomach trouble. In the bathroom I removed my boots and carried out instructions.

John, meanwhile, had raised the temperature in the kitchen to the low hundreds Fahrenheit here and below, and was experimenting with a scraper on the wall with some success. The drying bread came off quite easily, but so did the underlying green distemper (an early, cheap, version of emulsion paint) leaving swirls of grey undercoat. Quite trendy, really, in a later age.

Then nemesis struck. Mom arrived back early. She appeared suddenly through the back door, straight into her super-heated kitchen, truly a Hell's Kitchen, to find her eldest son scraping the walls, everything covered in grey goo (with an occasional currant), the mangle open with a split pillowcase dangling from its lips and an outline of a small boy's torso on the opposite wall.

Afterwards, it was rumoured that Mom's wail of anguish was heard three streets away, and the thump she awarded John's head was discerned in the local park.

"Where's Eric?" she asked, looking fearfully at my outline as if I had been atomised.

"In the bathroom, cleaning up," said John.

"It's not bath night," said Mom sharply. Then she added, darkly, "There's something going on here."

With this masterly understatement she rushed upstairs (Mom never walked, she always ran.) She burst into the bathroom and stopped abruptly, stunned by the second shock of the day. Her younger son, who had misheard instructions lay, fully clothed, submerged in the bathwater on which floated the ever present diluted bread mix (with an occasional currant) vigorously shaking his head to dislodge the plugs in his ears whilst snorting, seal fashion, to clear his nose. His boots were neatly placed beside the bath.

This time, Mom's wail could be heard in the Bull Ring in Birmingham, and several ducks in Canon Hill Park thought the noise was a portent of winter winds and took flight to North Africa. I was hauled out of the bath, stripped and dried, and ordered to join my brother in the kitchen, which I rapidly did, clutching a towel for modesty purposes. Mom was even quicker as she followed me, sliding on my previous trail and missing the odd stair.

John and I huddled together amidst the scene of devastation.

"So, what in God's name were you up to?" shouted Mom.

"John did it," I opined.

"We were cooking something for you," John said.

Mom went a funny colour and strangled sounds came from her throat. "Cooking?" she gargled.

To calm the atmosphere, which was still quite oppressive, I tried to change the subject.

"What's for tea, Mom?" I enquired, brightly.

Mom turned a smouldering look on me.

"I cooked it last night, to save time today," she said.

"Oh, good – where is it?" I asked, looking around at the debris.

"In the cupboard over the stove; not that you two are getting any," she replied.

"Oh Mom, I'm hungry," I wailed, "what is it?"

"Bread pudding," said Mom.

8. SHOCK TACTICS

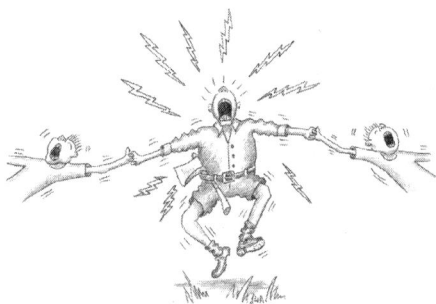

We were terrorised on our council estate by one young person, nominally a boy but really an Anthropoid named 'Chopper Smith'. He didn't have a Christian name, as the description didn't fit him somehow. It wasn't just his ape-like gait which frightened us or his sagging features – of which he had many – but his habit of carrying a chopper. He was an outstanding eccentric, in an area which had oddities by the dozen.

Chopper Smith was our resident fire-raiser, who called regularly when parents were out, drunk or missing, and demanded firewood that was in short supply. If none was forthcoming he would chop the top bar off your garden gate and lope off with it to light a fire, sometimes against one's fence. Gates in our vicinity always looked forlorn and unloved, as Chopper Smith slowly reduced them in stature.

To avoid confrontation with Chopper Smith, we got into the swing of things by directing him to the nearest ruin of any house on the estate which had been smashed during the frequent German bombing raids; preferably still smoking. There, Chopper Smith would gleefully re-ignite the remains and caper about in mindless ecstasy.

Nobody dared to complain, as Chopper Smith's dad was a coalman with a mighty torso developed through years of carrying tons of coal, a hundredweight at a time, up countless alleys to gaping coal holes. This fearsome man was often drunk and, if anyone annoyed him or inadvertently opposed him, would render the unfortunate man comatose with one terrible blow, then pick him up and carry him around seeking a suitable place to throw him – such as the nearby Grand Union Canal or the disused sewage farm.

Big Brother John, two years senior to my eight, swore solemnly to avenge himself against the constant humiliations handed out by Chopper Smith. Thus it was that one day John uttered the chilling word "IDEA!"

My heart did its usual plunge as I contemplated disaster and the limited future which this foretold.

John's revenge involved using his new invention, a magneto – or sort of crude car dynamo rescued from a bombed-out vehicle. This part normally fed electric current to sparkplugs when its interior was rotated. John used to wire up one side of brass doorknobs, where he crouched awaiting his victim like a polar bear at an ice-hole. When one approached the other side of the door, he would rotate his infernal machine by way of a bicycle pedal attached to the side and, as your hand grasped the opposing doorknob, a surge of direct current would shoot up your arm and paralyse your muscles.

The shock was severe and memorable and, for years afterwards, when grasping doorknobs (or coffin handles) I always covered my hand by pulling down my jersey sleeve or using hastily yanked out shirt-tails.

John explained his plan which, as ever, contained a grain of genius amongst the chaff of calamity. We were to collect a group of young children who would be told that we were going to form a fairy ring by all holding hands, and we would also tell them that when they felt a tickle in their palms a Good Wizard would appear, bearing gifts of toys and bananas. Nobody had seen a banana for years in 1942 so this was the clincher.

I objected, saying that we didn't have gifts or bananas. John eyed me with the disdain of Genghis Khan. He replied that, in that case, we would tell them that the magic was being performed at the wrong time of day and that we would give them each an apple.

"But we haven't got any apples," I protested.

"No, but our neighbour's tree has," said John, irrefutably.

The children were rounded up and soon formed an excited circle, bless them. They knew not what they did, and held hands. At this point, Chopper Smith lurched into view and demanded to know what was afoot. Now John's genius was apparent. He told him that we were performing magic and would summon a wizard bearing gifts for the children, but that he, Chopper Smith, could not join in. On being told this Chopper Smith was, of course, much angered and barged his way in, shoving his chopper in his belt and grabbing the hands of two terrified mites.

"OK! Magic us," said he, which was the longest sentence he ever managed.

John produced his magic machine, which had been embellished with two chromium-plated tubes, hack-sawn off the handlebars of a nearby bike left momentarily unattended, which were wired to the electric terminals of the magneto. At a nod from John I put these shiny toys into the eager hands of two adjacent toddlers and hurriedly stood back. John turned the handle, very slowly, and a murmur of excitement rose from the circle as their little extremities experienced a tiny tickle. Then, with a grin that Lucifer would have envied, to summon the Wizard John ordered the congregation to sing 'Old Macdonald had a Farm'.

At the appropriate moment, as they began to sing John increased the revolutions to the maximum he could manage and the song copied him – "Old Macdonald had a Farm, ee, aye, ee, aye – AARGH!" As the surge of electricity snaked around the fairy ring the tots screamed as the shock hit them – and they couldn't let go their hands.

Chopper Smith was a joy to behold. He screamed and jumped, he foamed and frothed; he sparked and went a funny colour.

"Beg for Mercy," ordered John.

"Murphy, Murphy…" was all he could manage.

"Tell me I'm the Emperor of Dalston Road," ordered John.

"'Mprer 'Alston 'Erd," blubbed Chopper Smith.

The handle ceased to turn, the survivors dropped to the pavement like discards in the Rag Market, and the dazed and defeated Chopper Smith staggered off to look for a tree where he could rest in the branches.

The tots collected themselves and scampered home, shakily. John and I stood proudly erect; we had done it. Chopper Smith was vanquished forever. We were free men and John was Emperor, albeit of one street. Quietude descended, but not for long.

Reluctantly we went home and told Mom, who anticipated trouble as the little ones returned to their mothers. Mom dished out the required thumps to our heads, and enquired about John's machine. He explained the workings, and we went outside to face the foe.

Quite quickly a grey posse of mothers arrived, headed by Mrs. Smith, and advanced up the garden path to face Mom who stood squarely in our doorway, arms akimbo.

"Your son has nearly killed my son…"

She got no further. Mom stood close to Mrs. Smith and

yelled at her.

"Pity they didn't finish the job. Your son wouldn't be here if you hadn't copulated with a passing dray horse." (I paraphrase).

This drew a reaction from the posse; most were shocked but some looked with new interest at Mrs. Smith. Without pause Mom continued for five minutes in similar vein – learned from her father, a master butcher – sometimes in incomprehensible backslang. She paused dramatically and turned to John:

"Where's this electric machine?" she demanded.

John produced it.

"How far does it reach?"

"Mm, about fifty yards Mom," John replied, pointing the chrome tubes at the grey crowd. He started to turn the handle...

That was breakpoint. The posse turned and fled. The exodus through the wreck of our gate, thoughtfully enlarged by Mrs. Smith's offspring, made Dunkirk look well organised. When the gateway became blocked, they fought and scratched their way through the privet hedge on either side and fanned out into the roadway to escape imminent electrocution, quickly returning to their homes to wallop their little ones for getting them into the dispute, and began to cook tea for their lords and countless children.

Mom went back inside the house. John and I grinned at each other; once again quietude descended, but not for long.

9. GAMES OF CHANCE
& 'PENNY-ON-THE-BRICK'

During the grim and grimy early months of the Second World War, many men were in reserved occupations as they transferred their skills to the production of munitions.

Vast pre-war motor car, motorbike and allied trades were converted to make guns, shells, tanks and 'planes in their tens of thousands. Birmingham, the capital city of metal bashers; the city of a thousand trades, settled down to supply the Armed Forces with anything they wanted – provided it was made of metal.

The workers' hours were long and arduous and they arrived home often late and tired. But their day wasn't finished; they then took up duties as ARP wardens and firewatchers. Their only respite was woodbine cigarettes and weak beer.

During those black days of constant bombardment by the

German bombers, the children were expected to keep quiet and '...don't bother your father.' Consequently, the streets were awash with children in the early evening, free from parental control – not so much neglected as discarded. Although wife and child beatings were commonplace, abuse was unheard of and every child was the responsibility of every woman. At that time there were many large families, where children with absent fathers were produced by spontaneous conception.

Thus were sown the seeds of innovative games amongst the evolving gangs, sometimes dangerous but always exhilarating, where leaders appeared who simulated the exploits of villains seen at Saturday morning matinees at the 'Pictures' (never cinemas). It is noteworthy that propaganda amongst unsupervised children always has the opposite effect. Show them Nazis brutalising civilians with heroes rescuing them and they will usually copy the Nazis.

We explored sulphurous bomb craters for the precious metal called shrapnel, which was very swappable. As usual John had a bright 'IDEA' and took me, quavering, to Yardley cemetery which we entered by clambering over the walls as the iron railings had been removed for melting down. He pointed out that, although the gravel-covered graves were overgrown, shrapnel could easily be found from craters where bombs had missed surrounding factory targets. Thereafter we were frequently to be seen scavenging amongst the 'Dear Departed' and 'Sadly Missed' slabs and headstones.

This practice was banned after we found a still-smoking incendiary device, which we proudly took home - where, to much alarm, it was noticed that the bomb had not detonated, and ARP wardens rapidly evacuated our house and street. John strongly objected when the bomb was confiscated and placed in a bucket of water.

"It's a dud," he explained. "'Nickle Eck' (my family nickname) dropped it twice and it didn't explode."

We would sometimes dump ill-behaved tots into emergency water tanks to test their innate aquatic abilities, or shut them into large metal waste paper bins with the lids closed, and then bash the sides with sticks. The resultant cacophony rendered the victim disorientated, speechless and dazed for days.

Polly-on-the-Mop-Stick was played with two teams of equal size. The first team leader would grasp the top bar of a suitable fence and his team would form a long mop stick behind him, bending over to firmly hold the haunches of the one in front. When all were settled, the opposing 'Pollies' team would scream battle cries and race towards the wavering mop stick, hurling themselves one by one along its length to cling on and commence riding, using their heels in approved cowboy style. If the swaying, overloaded 'beast' could stay upright whilst chanting 'Polly-on the-Mop-Stick' they threw off their tormentors and swapped places.

This merry pastime was eventually banned by grown-ups, who complained either about their demolished fences and hedges or their damaged offspring, some of whom could be seen wandering about moaning, "Me back, me back," often with their heads at an odd angle and their faces turning a funny colour.

A nearby ruined Gothic mansion, survivor of Acocks Green's rural past, was a paradise for our adventures: parachute jumps off bay window tops, jungle warfare in the old orchard and spectacular mountaineering up beams and balustrades on either side of staircases which lacked stairs.

There was a majestic chestnut tree in the grounds, disdainfully towering to eighty feet overlooking the new estates around it. In particular, it possessed a powerful lower limb. The outer small branches and leafy twigs could be reached from the ground, and the whole limb could be slowly bent down by armies of children, some of whom clambered aboard and rode the 'rearing and plunging beast' as it was released from the ground.

Everyone wanted to have a go, and everyone was satisfied – but for one snot-begrimed toddler who was too small to hold on. His constant whining of "'Ave go! 'ave go!" eventually persuaded the leaders to shut him up, by allowing him a turn and to teach him a lesson. The limb was bent down, the grimy tot placed in the twigs at the end, and the leaders climbed aboard. The tethered ride was freed from ground control and commenced to thrash its way to freedom. At its lowest mighty sway, a signal was given and all the leaders jumped off.

The freed branch shuddered and whipped up, catapulting the tiny tot into the unknown blue yonder. We watched in open-mouthed awe as the tot rose in parabolic perfection, his clutching fingers grasping air until he dwindled into a small speck in the sky.

Time slowed down. The ten-year-old elders of the tribe gathered to discuss the situation. Grave comments were made, culled from *Marvel* comics begged from American servicemen passing through:

"There ain't any oxygen up there."

"His eyes will pop out."

"His head will explode."

"When he hits the ground he'll make a great crater."

Several warriors remembered pressing appointments elsewhere and left the field of conflict, in anticipation of the wrath of the mother of the babe-in-space. The rest of us rushed over to stand under the projected re-entry flight path of the infant astronaut, and mercifully caught him in our upraised hands as he crashed through the leafy twigs of our lovely tree.

He never again asked to "'Ave go!"

*

'Penny-on-the-Brick' was without doubt our family favourite.

John, my elder brother by two insurmountable years, and our 'adopted brother' Edward (strangely, never Ted) coerced for the occasion, gathered at dusk on Saturday evenings and hid amongst the dark under-belly of our house's massive privet hedge fronting the street. I thought the hedge was so-called because it gave privacy to the homestead. We set out our equipment, which consisted of three house bricks laid side by side amongst the roots, and a penny.

We crouched with silent Apache patience to await the return of the unsteady patrons of the local pubs. We would pick a small group of murmuring men (never women) and as they approached we calculated their speed and held the penny above the bricks; not too high as it would bounce off, not too low or it would lack resonance – but just so... and as they trudged past we dropped the penny, which tinkled realistically. The group paused. Consternation; someone had dropped some change on to the pavement!

With barely suppressed glee we listened and watched as everyone counted the change in their pockets and then commenced scouring the area and the gutter for the missing coin. Some got down on their knees and carefully swept the ground with their hands; money was tight and it could be half-a-crown which had been dropped. This modus operandi brought their faces to within inches of our concealed bodies and froze us into a breathless hush. Eventually they gave up and plodded homeward to a mixed reception from their spouses.

Our joy was unrestrained, especially on those occasions when following groups joined in the search so that it seemed that the residents of the whole street were searching, as they turned Dalston Road into a Klondike cursing mob digging for golden change. All this for a penny – on a brick.

The grand finale of this particular game was memorable for its simplicity. One evening we selected a group of returning inebriates which contained a young man who had been out drinking with his dad and who, unfortunately for us, had participated in Penny-on-the-Brick in his youth.

Without preamble he immediately peed through the privet hedge with wide sweeps to encompass us all. We naturally let out cries of protest, at which point the young man rushed round to our side of the garden, picked us up and deposited us into the massive privet hedge – the thickness of which was welcoming but reluctant to release its prisoners.

Eventually we emerged much chastened, scratched and smelling unsociably.

I looked at the state of the privet hedge. "That's going to take some explaining," I thought and determined never again to play that particular game.

10. FRED'S ENTERPRISE

Our younger brother, Fred, was always eager to make money. His main income was arranging puppet shows in the garden on a homemade stage consisting of wood and cardboard. Children sat around the stage and paid two pence each for his show. The puppets were made up and painted, and Fred provided the off-stage voices.

To get more money for a bike, Fred decided he needed a more professional show, so he set about making his characters from paper mâché. He mixed the necessary paper until it reached the right consistency and then created his puppets as gnomes, fairies, crocodiles, Punch & Judy, and the monster. After they were created he left them overnight to dry in front of the fire. The next morning we heard a terrible noise, and ran downstairs to find that the dog had chewed up all the puppets! Fred screamed, cried, and threatened to kill the dog, while John and I laughed for days; John thought he could have made more money by showing the audience a sketch showing what the dog had done.

He made another troupe of puppets but made sure the dog was in his kennel at night. Eventually Fred got his bike, but there was another howling fit when someone stole it!

*

Fred had a great pal named Edward (never Ted), who has remained a family friend throughout our lives, and we considered him to be an 'honorary brother'. They would get up to mischief too. Their chief preoccupation was smoking, but this had to be done secretly without Mom's knowledge. The boys spent a lot of time at Edward's house where one day they came across a tin of 'tobacco' in the kitchen. They bought some cigarette papers and proceeded to 'roll their own', quickly disappearing to a hiding place where they smoked all afternoon. Big mistake! They were surprised at how popular smoking was with most of their male relatives, as the cigarettes had a horrible taste and the boys were terribly sick, putting them off smoking for a while – until all was revealed when Edward's mum was heard to cry in exasperation, "Who's been messing with my sage and onion stuffing?"

This experience didn't put Fred and Edward off, and they continued to smoke with some genuine cigarettes they had pilfered.

In a nearby park, a number of trees had been lopped as it was an area for barrage balloons, and there was a danger of the securing ropes getting entangled in the branches. One of the remaining trees was a favourite for Fred and Edward to climb, and they enjoyed secret smoking sessions from their lair near the top, carelessly tossing away the stubs from time to time.

One evening someone excitedly reported a strange sight; a tree seemed to be illuminated near the top. Curiously, Fred and Edward mingled with a group of neighbours who had gathered with interest to view the phenomenon; then it dawned on them – a cigarette stub had been smouldering all day, and eventually the tree caught fire.

The fire brigade was called and by now a large crowd gathered, eager to see what was going on. Fred and Edward were amongst a group of boys who were sternly questioned as to whether they knew anything about it, but Edward maintained he couldn't climb trees, and the policeman moved on. Much to their relief they were never punished, but they had to find another place for their illicit smoking sessions.

One Bonfire Night, Fred and Edward had their pockets full of "bangers" and mooched around wondering what to do with them. They came across an alleyway with a locked door at the end; zooming up to the door, they tossed the bangers over the top and sped off. As they ran, behind them was an explosion and the door blew off – revealing a gas meter behind it!

Another favourite game for these two involved a huge inner tube they had found, discarded from a large aircraft. They blew this up and, from their hideout up the tree, they threw it off the top branches, excitedly straining to watch it bounce. At that moment Grandma came into view, carrying her shopping bag, but it was too late; the tube was on its way, bouncing up high and down again, missing her by inches. Grandma stopped the astonished passers by, demanding to know how a plane could fly without one of its wheels.

11. EVACUATION

I was six years old and had never been away from home, nor had I been on a train. I was a very frightened boy waiting on the platform at Snow Hill Station, Birmingham in September 1939, as huge crowds of young evacuees swirled around me. Teachers shouted, children started crying and the engine of the great train steamed at every joint and emitted shattering shrieks from its giant whistle.

I was overwhelmed by the scene and clutched my brother John, my gas mask and a bag of cream crackers. My label over-identified me as 'Male boy, one of two' and gave my name, which only confused me further. I wondered what I was doing in this inferno of noise and chaos...

The Government's Evacuation Scheme was a result of escalating civilian casualties in London and other manufacturing cities during the German Blitzkrieg. Rural areas were ordered to provide accommodation for thousands of children, and city families were encouraged to send their young children away to safer areas – but this was voluntary, not prescriptive. Thus, evacuation was born and has forever after become an emotive word to my generation.

Impetus was given to the scheme after a series of bombing raids on the Midlands during late 1940. The entire night shift of the BSA Munitions factory in the grimly-named Armoury Road, Birmingham, was killed after several direct hits. Entire streets of back-to-back houses were reduced to rubble. The middle of Coventry disappeared, leaving only the defiant smoking ruins of the Cathedral the following day.

One night, during the wail of the air raid siren our family raced from the house with pillows over our heads to the Anderson shelter in the front garden. I noticed glowing incendiaries in the street and a reddened sky in the background. We quickly settled down to await the 'All Clear' sound, but that night was a long one.

Mom suggested telling stories to pass the time. As I had the beginnings of a lifetime's love of acting I volunteered, and started my rendition of *The Three Little Pigs and The Big Bad Wolf*. Everything went well until I reached the wolf's immortal line, 'If you don't come out I'll huff and I'll puff and I'll BLOW YOUR HOUSE DOWN.' My audience was unimpressed with my performance and I lapsed into a hurt silence; who were they to complain, they hadn't bought a ticket.

The mood perceptively changed. Hundreds of bodies were pulled from the demolished houses, some still burning horribly after being hit by fragments of phosphorous incendiary bombs. The Emergency Council decided to concrete over the BSA factory ruins to create a mass grave memorial. Thousands of quietly grieving widows queued outside the remaining munitions factories to offer their labour as replacements for their dead men. Children were then registered for evacuation. Burials were hastily arranged.

The organisation was very good. Children were gathered in schools and halls, often between the air raids. Buses were sequestered and trains were marshalled. Dispersal villages and towns were put on stand-by. The story of this monumentally successful enterprise has not yet been told – except by vignettes from the evacuees.

So John and I, together with hundreds of others on the platform, were told that if we wanted 'to leave the room' we must go now, as it would not be possible 'to go' on the train. We all trooped off to inadequate lavatories where the boys peed against any flat surface, inside and outside. How the girls managed has not been recorded. We were then herded into carriages and packed tightly into rows, with one teacher for each compartment, and our adventure began.

I studied the pictures kindly provided by the management of Great Western Railways (G.W.R.). They all depicted families cavorting amongst sandcastles on sunny beaches under blue skies, with not a Spitfire in sight.

Our teacher led us in choral singing and we learnt the words of *Old Macdonald had a Farm* and *Green Grow the Rushes O!* John and I joined in half-heartedly. Neither of us then, nor later, enjoyed community happenings – unless John was in charge. I tried to eat my snack, but found it impossible to sing and eat cream crackers. John silently brushed flakes of cream crackers off his shorts and gave me a look which could have been used instead of ammunition at Rourkes Drift.

We arrived tired and dispirited at Retford, near Nottingham. It was an unlovely little town where nothing happened, very slowly. Historically it had once been a 'rotten borough', sending a nominated MP to Westminster as they had no electors. The term suited its ambience.

We were ushered into a large hall where we were met by crowds of prospective foster parents, and Registry Officers whom we would meet frequently. There followed an inspection of the children which would have impressed Arab slave traders in the Sudan. My hair was combed for nits, teeth viewed for rot and my skimpy arms for muscle. I was even asked by one Faginesque creature if I had "any impediments?"

Not knowing what an impediment was, I replied in my jagged Brummie accent, "No, just me suitcase."

Finally John and I were allocated to a middle-class couple who really wanted two little girls. Not a propitious start. At their comfortable home we were shown to our room with twin beds, which we had not seen before, and given a meal. This was strange as well; the Yorkshire pudding was served separately, so I thought that was all there was and got up to leave. I was assured there was more to come and ate the other courses quickly. There did seem to be a lot of spare cutlery on the table but I left it unused to save on washing up.

After dinner John and I sat on a sofa and gazed at the couple across an un-bridgeable culture gulf. We didn't last long there, as we often returned from school dishevelled and bruised from fights with local boys. I became something of a junior champion as various bullies tormented me during the dinner break. I wasn't very strong but I was quick, and could often damage my opponents by concentrating my punches on their stomachs which contained recently ingested food. Inevitably bigger boys beat me up if I looked like winning.

The Billeting Officer then sent us to lodge with an elderly couple called Golland, who must have needed the money.

We shared our attic room with a youngish woman who appeared each night after we had gone to bed. She never put the light on but undressed in the dark, discarding about seventeen garments. A large bowl of assorted nuts was then pulled out from under her bed, and we drifted off to sleep to the sound of cracking shells and grinding molars. Each morning she would be long gone, leaving evidence of a monkey's meal behind her.

"Funny woman," I remarked.

"A nutter," said John. Ah! He was so witty.

In an old outhouse one day we found dusty bottles of homemade elderberry wine. The description 'wine' we thought a little presumptuous considering its humble origin, but amusing enough. We got into the habit of swigging a few mouthfuls now and then and replacing the missing quantity with tap water. The 'wine' was sweet and made us feel squiffy for a while – and bolder, with disastrous consequences.

Mr. Golland was a very keen gardener, somewhat constrained by a gammy leg which caused him to use a walking stick. We often helped him, but only with mundane tasks like weeding or watering the pots in his greenhouse. This greenhouse had a brick base about three feet high, surmounted by the usual glass and wooden framed top, with only one narrow door.

One day, growing tired of watering the individual pots, John suddenly exclaimed, "IDEA!"

My heart contracted and my breathing became shallow. John's ideas always worked, after a fashion, but I usually came to grief.

"Wha'?" I enquired, trying not to sound too keen.

"Water the greenhouse," John replied, pointing to the brick surround. "We'll put the hose pipe through a broken window into the base, jam the door tight with cardboard, turn the water on and - after a while - the level will reach the pots and do the job automatically."

After a few swigs of elderberry wine I was game for anything.

We lined the potted plants up on slatted staging, put the hose pipe along the floor, jammed the door and turned the water on. The level was slow at first as the water soaked into the gravel floor, but soon the depth increased. We watched fascinated as the brick base turned into an indoor swimming pool and lapped at the bottom of the pots.

"That's enough," said John, "turn the water off."

I hurried to the tap and met Mr. Golland on his way to the

greenhouse.

"What are you two up to?" he asked.

"We're watering your plants and cleaning the shelves," I replied loudly, to give warning to John who was removing the hosepipe.

Mr. Golland sniffed and said that he would inspect our work. He hobbled onward as John and I stopped breathing and watched, frozen with horror, as he grabbed the door knob and pulled. The door stuck. Mr Golland was having none of this; he put his stick over one arm and, using both hands, gave a mighty heave. The door crashed open and a huge rolling wave engulfed him. Frothing whitecaps lapped round him as he surfed past on his way to his supper, surrounded by bobbing plants and his stick.

"This is going to take some explaining," I thought.

Amazingly, Mr. Golland accepted that we had accidentally left the hosepipe on. We retrieved the pots and his stick, and begged his forgiveness. I did my wide-eyed innocent cherubic act, and John reminded him that the greenhouse wouldn't need cleaning out for some time.

As Mr. Golland went towards the house to change, John pointed out that he should really be quite pleased, as we had watered the whole garden as well as the pots. This intelligence was greeted by another sniff as Mr. Golland went inside.

All would have ended, if not well, at least amicably had Mr. Golland not sent his wife to the outhouse for a bottle of her elderberry wine to help his recovery from the storm-tossed sea. John and I stared at each other. The wine by now was much diluted and was merely pink water. We didn't wait for the repercussions but postponed the inevitable return of the Billeting Officer by going for a long walk in nearby Nottingham Forest.

The forest was our solace, where we could escape and be free from bullies and nagging old people. Here we learned to supplement our meagre diet. Elderly foster parents always fed us, but they had no understanding of the gigantic appetites of growing youngsters, who are always hungry.

We fed in season off sweet chestnuts and cobnuts. We snuffled like truffle pigs for pignuts growing in the roots of trees. Dandelion leaves became salads and the fresh spring growth of hawthorn shoots became bread and cheese.

Nectar in small quantities came from many wild flowers and blackberries and elderberries filled our demanding stomachs. Sometimes we were lost, but the forest was always benign – except once when I walked too near the water's edge of a lake and began to sink into a quagmire. John coolly found a fallen branch which reached my disappearing figure, and slowly and with much squelching he pulled me out of the enveloping mud.

I gazed in horror at my thickly-coated boots and socks. What could I do? In desperation I tried to disguise them with grey dust and returned home to secretly clean myself up. I almost got away with it, but for the black trail I left across the kitchen floor which, not surprisingly, attracted some attention.

It has always puzzled me why adults address miscreant children with the phrase, "What on earth were you thinking of?" Don't they know? Children – especially boys – never think and are quite unacquainted with consequences. I was chastised, but not overly.

Subsequently we were returned to the Billeting Officer, who by now was running out of foster parents who hadn't heard of our adventurous spirit. After rejecting Stalag Luft IV as being too soft, he sent us to a lady who would take any miscreant for the lodging allowance. She lived in a flat in an area called Spittlefields, which gives an idea of its ambience.

Here we shared a large bed with six other rejects who slept sardine fashion, three heads at the top and three at the bottom. We endured a certain amount of bullying so we stayed outside as much as possible, our favourite haunt being the nearby canal.

This waterway had a splendid overflow weir next to a lock. We had tried to dam it but couldn't manage heavy stones, so had to be content with removing and dumping the 'Danger' sign above the flow, to confuse and drown any German paratroopers advancing in rubber boats.

There were many varieties of fish in the lock, but we didn't catch many with our bent pins and bread bait. One day I sorrowfully pointed out to John that it would be easier to see and catch more fish if the water wasn't so deep. I should have known better.

"IDEA!" said John.

My heart performed its usual contraction. I said a silent farewell to the world and prepared to drown myself.

"If we let some of the water out of the lock," John explained, "we will then catch the fish in the shallows – with nets." He looked at me triumphantly.

I was about to ask where we could get nets from when prudence overcame me. John would probably use my vest.

We tackled the downstream gates which had a huge handle. When turned the thick boards at the bottom would lift to allow the lock to slowly empty, thus freeing the gates to open inwards. After Homeric efforts we raised the boards about a foot and waited for the waters to abate. After about half an hour the lock was still full but the water was pouring out under the gates. We were perplexed. We then noted that the surface of the lock water was flowing like a river.

Understanding crept slowly into our brains. We looked anxiously at each other, perhaps for the last time as free men, and then stoically looked upstream. Those gates which we had overlooked were crookedly still open – and we were engaged in draining the upper canal into the lower one.

The lower reaches were soon inundated and we were questioned by several damp farmers and the police. Ultimately, we were summoned to appear before Magistrates in the local Juvenile Court.

John was highly pleased with this turn of events and in the local library he started to bone up on Great Victorian Trials. Mysteriously, he also had our hair cut short at a back street barber shop run by a misanthrope who had the same attitude to children as King Herod had held once upon a time.

We then retrieved the 'Danger' sign and placed it in an alley next to the police station (easily done in the dark when no street lights were permitted); we were ready.

John gave me my orders. "Shurrup and agree with me!"

The Juvenile Court was held in the Main Court, as there was nowhere else available. Apparently Juvenile crime was very rare until we hit town.

The Clerk of the court explained the procedure, as kindly as he could, and put us in the dock – which was rather intimidating as there were spikes at the front and I couldn't see over the top.

I looked up at the Bench and saw an elderly man with white hair, a grey moustache and purple cheeks, who told us in strangled vowels that this was a 'hearing' not a trial, and that he was the Magistrate (juvenile) and he would be assisted by two assessors – indicating the occupants of high backed chairs on either side of him.

These two assessors were so very aged and shrunken that it was impossible to tell their sex; they were probably interchangeable. Their faces were so wrinkled that their eyes had sunk deep into their heads and it appeared that they could only open them one at a time.

The hearing commenced with the Magistrate asking if we were two brothers, John and Eric. The Bench peered at us with four eyes, two in the middle and one either side. They were understandably perplexed as they could only see John.

"Ahem! Where is your brother?" he was asked.

"Stand on your toes," hissed John and, as I did so, he grabbed my jacket collar and lifted me up.

"Present," he said.

"Quite so, quite so," said the Magistrate and nodded at his two acolytes who shrank back into the chairs' upholstery and nodded off.

The police gave their version of events, which sounded as if thousands of acres were flooded, cows swept out to sea, industry destroyed and dear little children and their widowed mothers rescued from rooftops.

The Court was silent. All this mayhem caused by John and his invisible brother! We were doomed.

I was grateful to John for helping me to strengthen my neck muscles against the tightening of the hangman's noose. But I had underestimated him and he had done his homework well.

"What is your explanation for these events?" the Magistrate enquired.

John stood tall and straightened his imaginary wig and gown. "M'Lud…" he started, but was interrupted.

"Don't call me 'M'Lud,'" the Magistrate interposed, "I'm not a Judge."

"Right," said John, "your Highness…" again his rhetoric was interrupted.

"Sir," said the Clerk of the Court.

"Yes?" said John, turning towards him.

The Magistrates' Clerk went a deeper purple.

"We are not calling *you* 'Sir' – you should address the Magistrate as 'Sir'."

"Right, Sir," said John, "the defence case rests on

mistaken identity, alibis and negligence."

The Court was riveted. The Police Officer's eyebrows elevated somewhat, the assessors opened an eye each, my hidden mouth opened and stayed that way and the Magistrate sighed at the prospect of a late lunch.

"Be so kind as to explain," he intoned.

"Right M'Lud," said John. The Magistrate gave up and John explained to an increasingly bemused Bench, in his thick Birmingham accent, the circumstances leading to our unwarranted incarceration. He pointed out in fine detail that:

Isambard Kingdom Brunel's design of the lock was flawed because:

The lower gate sluices should not be capable of opening until the upper gates were shut and, furthermore, the mechanisms were badly neglected and had not been maintained, which was contrary to The Minister of War's instructions that all canals MUST (and here John thumped the spiked ledge of the dock and repeated, MUST) be kept in good order to maintain the flow of material destined for The War Effort. We had only drained three miles, not hundreds as the police alleged, and (realising that this might be construed as a confession, he hurried on) in fact, we were innocent bystanders who were a mile away having our hair cut. Here, John inclined his bristly head and hauled me on to my toes to display my stubbly swede to the public gaze. Finally he declared that there should be a 'Warning' sign near the weir to prevent vulnerable little children like us from being swept away (John had reached his peroration and pointed dramatically at the dumbfounded Police Officer), so why was this aforementioned sign sitting in an alley next to the police station?

"I rest my case Your Highness," John concluded.

The Court stirred; nothing this exciting had happened in Retford since Robin Hood had redistributed local income.

The Magistrate knew that he had been stitched up and that

the allegations of neglect might cause trouble to 'The Powers That Be'. He addressed the Constable,

"Is this 'Warning' sign at your police station?"

"Er, yes Your Worship. We found it outside but didn't know what to do with it," replied the Constable.

"And what is printed on it?" he was asked.

"'Danger – Weir' Your Worship," the Constable answered reluctantly.

The Magistrate glared at him and I grinned at John.

After conferring with the two crones on the Bench he told us that, under the circumstances outlined by John, we would not be punished. However, for the safety of Retford we must be separated and dwell apart.

"Case dismissed," he concluded.

I was carried away crying and screaming for my brother, who strode away triumphant and stern faced, as befitted such a renowned Q.C. – my brother John, aged 11 years.

*

My final billet was with an attractive woman whom I shall call Pearl, as she fronted eight swine-like evacuees who all resided with her in a 'two-up and two-down' terraced house. These children were the dregs of the system; none of them could be contained within normal households and many behaved like the protagonists in Lord of the Flies.

Pearl took her five shillings (*25p*) per head and guaranteed the Evacuation Registrars that there would be NO TROUBLE! An exhausted and untrained Evacuation Committee agreed with such terms and I was allowed to dwell therein. No doubt the committee anticipated that I would be subdued by separation from my brother, John, and the strictness of dear Pearl, but they seriously underestimated me – after all I was now eight years old and full of John's wise words.

The resident 'Flies' took an immediate dislike to me. I was sullen, uncooperative and unimpressed by threats and intimidation. In vain I was threatened with dire punishment if I did not conform to the diktat of their leader Joe, an ugly overgrown vegetable. Joe did not understand that he was talking to an opponent who, together with his brother John, had had the skin on his back whipped and shredded with a stripped branch from a privet hedge, wielded by a drunken and embittered father, for 'stealing' a radish from a neighbour's garden. Joe would learn that the brain is mightier than the swear word.

The food in our lodging was acceptable – plenty of greyish bread and potatoes, which provided much needed carbohydrates, and tinned sugary plum jam – readily available in the war years. Sleeping arrangements were of the tinned sardine variety, three bigger boys sleeping at the top of a large double bed with three smaller boys at the bottom. Joe and another boy slept in a single bed. This system kept us all warm and we all caught the same diseases at the same time.

Entertainment was simple – me! Apparently each newcomer was automatically designated a rodent, to be hunted every evening through the back streets of Retford. Dear Pearl entertained her men friends each evening – except on Sundays – and required us all to vacate the premises. I wondered for a while how she entertained her guests, and finally concluded that she sang to them.

To commence the procedure I was told to show my collection of glass marbles, one of my few possessions, as I was good at the game. As I proffered my marbles in a cupped hand Joe would kick my arm, to send the marbles flying in all directions. I refused to complain, cry or remonstrate. Instead I gathered up whatever marbles I could find and gazed without expression at my tormentors.

Frustrated at my lack of evident terror (although I was inwardly quaking) Joe told me that I was to be hunted through the streets by his followers and, when tracked down, I would be suitably punished. To be fair, he said if I could avoid his pack for two hours (loud jeers from his dribbling hounds) I would be pardoned for that evening.

I was to be given two minutes start – but as nobody had a watch I knew that time was not of the essence.

Poor Joe! Was I not the brother of John the Genius? Was I not a warrior of eight years of age? Was I not the possessor of an organ which Joe had been born without – a brain?

I asked what the punishment would be if I was caught. Joe replied I would be dumped in the water butt outside our billet (loud cheers from the horde) and off I fled.

I ran circuitously round the back streets, returning to our billet – and clambered into the water butt. There wasn't much water in the bottom and I removed my boots; I didn't have any socks. To pass the time I practised my 'Donald Duck' impressions, which John and I had been rehearsing for many months in order to beguile bullies and big boys. Eventually Joe and his followers returned, bewailing their lost prey (unaware I was already in the water butt) and threatening what they would do to me tomorrow, the day after that, and endless 'tomorrows'.

After a suitable interval, when all was quiet and Pearl had finished her repertoire of jolly songs, I crept into the billet and wriggled into my one-sixth portion of the bed.

This routine continued for several nights, Joe and his followers becoming increasingly frustrated and threatening. I then decided that the situation warranted a strategic withdrawal. The next night I waited, shivering in my water butt, and when the pack neared the billet I began to recite nursery rhymes in the voice of Donald Duck. This phenomenon stunned the hunters into silence and they crowded excitedly around the butt expecting to see a manifestation of Walt Disney's creation – only to find me.

Henceforth Joe decided that I was to be appointed the gang's jester and I was saved from further punishment. I did become heartily sick of rendering *'Baa Baa Blacksheep'* dozens of times as Donald Duck, but I survived.

Over two years had passed, during which we had no visits from Mom and Dad. After many letters home describing in awesome detail our misery and degradation, largely invented, John and I were reunited and returned to Birmingham where the air raids had diminished.

And so our adventures in Retford came to an end. It had been a time of growing up; a time of close lifetime bonding between two young brothers. It had been a time of increasing awareness that two little boys could defy a threatening world and survive, together.

AN ODE TO MY BROTHER

31 May 2011
(Following an operation)

Although your life is ticking,
The clock's in fabulous form
Its innards have had an MOT
And now you're back to norm.

If I could give you stem cells,
My gift would be so sweet
By sawing off your lower limbs
And giving you dainty feet.

You don't need changes to your brain
It's a wonder of the world
Bands go marching through the streets
With banners and flags unfurled.

My thanks for all you've taught me
I often reminisce -
Remembering those early years
When togetherness was bliss.

Through all our tribulations
In times long past and gone
My bestest pal stays in my heart
My Hero, Brother John.

'Nickle Eck'

EPITAPH TO 'NICKLE ECK'

19 March 2012

Remember our young years together
When the bombs rained down most of the nights?
We slept in an Anderson shelter
And the city shut down all its lights

With our gas masks and few small possessions
We travelled away from the Blitz
The train it ended at Retford
Where we started to live by our wits

Then we were forever together
With you always there at my side
Your little hand entwined in mine
Which was such a comforting sign

We were not very welcome at Retford
As we managed to empty their cut
The magistrates threatened us caning
But we struggled to keep our mouths shut

We roamed in the woods and the forests
Fished for hours with little success
Scrounged for food at market stalls
To try to assuage the hunger calls

We broke old Gal Golland's greenhouse
And managed to drink all her wine
I pushed you into a pond of mud
And you were all covered in slime

Now you are the one I look up to
Your intelligence sharp deep and wide
Your acting is simply quite brilliant
And I feel for you with great pride

You must forgive my childhood pranks
Electrocution, pain and stress
For you are the brother I love the most
Who has brought me great happiness

Your forever loving brother
John

Eric died on 12 April 2012
John died on 21 December 2013

ABOUT THE AUTHOR

Eric spent two years of his National Service as an Army Education Officer in Cyprus, and seven years with the Kenyan Police in East Africa where, as a Customs & Excise Investigation Officer, he swam in shark-infested waters looking for hidden contraband. Whilst living in Africa, where his daughter was born, he joined the National Theatre of Nairobi where he performed in the Classics, Shakespeare, drama, and pantomimes.

For almost 20 years he worked for Bass Charrington, controlling Licensed Premises throughout the Midlands, and also worked for Mitchells & Butlers in Birmingham, during which time he was with the Hall Green Little Theatre and became a stalwart member of the Blossomfield Club in Solihull, where for many years he performed, directed and was co-writer of original musical comedies produced and performed there. These included, *Julius* (Julius Caesar from the wives' viewpoint), *Long John Saliva* (Treasure Island), *One Over the Eight* (Snow White & the Seven Dwarfs), and *Oh, Blast* (based on the American *Moon Blast Mission*).

Eric became a presenter for BBC Radio Birmingham and spent ten years with the Monitoring Section of the BBC World Service in Berkshire, during which time he joined two esteemed Musical & Dramatic societies in Oxfordshire, becoming well-known for his acting talent, especially mimicry and humour, winning numerous awards over the years.

Eric was married twice with a son and a daughter from his first marriage and another son. He met his second wife in Henley-on-Thames, when she directed him as Henry Ormonroyd the photographer in J.B. Priestley's *When We Are Married*. At that time he was semi-retired working as a warden at Windsor Castle, where he endeared himself to his colleagues but was sometimes reprimanded for displaying his unique brand of humour to the general public.

Retiring to Devon in 2001, Eric filled his time with boat restoration, brewing very strong cider, cultivating rare trees and plants and reading anthologies, mathematical works and reference books on learned subjects. He began writing his stories in 2004 – and also began tales from his adult life, regrettably unfinished. Occasionally he and his wife performed in Salcombe, where he is celebrated in the South Hams for his performance in the famous music hall sketch 'Dinner for One' (YouTube – *Dinner for One, Eric*).

His final memorable performance was at the 2011 Dartmouth Drama Festival, five months before he died, where he brought the house down in the two miming sketches from Michael Frayn's *Alarms & Excursions*, directed by his wife. His expertise was as sharp as ever and, as always, he received tumultuous applause.

as HENRY ORMONROYD Photographer
in J. B. Priestley's 'WHEN WE ARE MARRIED'

N.O.D.A AWARD-NOMINATED PRODUCTION by
HENLEY-ON-THAMES OPERATIC & DRAMATIC
SOCIETY - FEBRUARY 1995

Directed by Lutena Meller

13468903R00060

Printed in Great Britain
by Amazon.co.uk, Ltd.,
Marston Gate.